Pitt Press Series

PLATONIS CRITO

CAMBRIDGE UNIVERSITY PRESS WAREHOUSE,

C. F. CLAY, Manager.

London: FETTER LANE, E.C.
Edinburgh: 100, PRINCES STREET.

Berlin: A. ASHER AND CO.
Leipzig: F. A. BROCKHAUS.
New York: G. P. PUTNAM'S SONS.
Bombay and Calcutta: MACMILLAN AND CO., Ltd.

PLATONIS CRITO

EDITED
WITH INTRODUCTION, NOTES AND GLOSSARY

BY
J. ADAM, Litt.D.

CAMBRIDGE:
AT THE UNIVERSITY PRESS
1908

ἐν εὐφημίᾳ χρὴ τελευτᾶν.

(PHAED. 117 D.)

CAMBRIDGE:
AT THE UNIVERSITY PRESS

First Edition, 1888.   *Reprinted* 1891, 1893, 1896, 1903, 1908,

TABLE OF CONTENTS.

PREFACE TO THE SECOND EDITION.

THE second edition has been revised throughout. I have been convinced by the arguments of several reviewers that my view of the difficult passage in 44 B requires modification, and I have modified it accordingly. In one or two other passages I have expressed myself (I hope) more clearly: otherwise there is no change.

I desire to thank the reviewers in England and in Germany for their courteous and considerate reception of this little work.

EMMANUEL COLLEGE,
 CAMBRIDGE,
  February 21, 1891.

PREFACE.

No apology is needed for a new edition of the Crito.
The only edition in English which possesses more than a
purely ephemeral value is Dyer's reproduction of Cron
(Boston, 1885). And to my mind the Crito is one of the
finest of Plato's minor dialogues, breathing the most ex-
alted morality, full of the deepest historical interest, and
above all (as I think I have shewn in my Introduction)
perfect as a work of art. As in the Apology, so here, I
have followed on the whole the readings of the Bodleian.
But I am as far as possible from wishing to disparage the
second family of manuscripts, and it will be seen from
my critical appendix that I have not infrequently preferred a reading traceable to it.

The editors to whom I am most indebted in the for-
mation of the text are Schanz and Kral: for the interpretation I have found Cron's edition far the most valuable.
I have also consulted the editions by Wohlrab and Göbel,
and other critical contributions to the study of the
dialogue referred to in my notes. But I have frequently

ventured to differ from the other editors in the interpretation of the dialogue: and a large part of the commentary is my own.

I have again gratefully to acknowledge my obligations to Mr Neil.

EMMANUEL COLLEGE,
November 25, 1887.

INTRODUCTION.

THE Crito is one of the Socratic tetralogy of dialogues, embracing the Euthyphro, the Apology, the Crito and the Phaedo. The justification for grouping these together is that each of them is concerned with the circumstances of Socrates' trial, imprisonment and death. At the outset of the Euthyphro, we are favoured with a description of Socrates' accuser, together with a brief account of the indictment: while in the rest of the dialogue Plato proceeds to refute by anticipation the charge of impiety, shewing how infinitely more reverent is the scepticism of Socrates than the unreflecting orthodoxy of which Euthyphro is the exponent. The Apology was intended by Plato to be a triumphant vindication of the whole faith and practice of his master in society, religion and politics. In the Crito and the Phaedo we are brought face to face with issues which are at once narrower and wider: narrower, inasmuch as they deal with one particular aspect of Socrates' personality, the Crito with his political, the Phaedo with his eschatological views, freely developed and expanded by Plato: wider, because in both we are introduced to problems of more universal interest, in the Crito to the relation between the individual and the State, in the Phaedo to the immortality of the soul.

If we regard the Euthyphro as a kind of prologue to the great trilogy of which Socrates is the central figure, we shall see in the Crito as it were the second drama, related to the first and last much as the Choephori is related to the Agamemnon and the Eumenides. From one point of view, indeed, there might seem to be a closer connection between the Crito and the Phaedo than between it and the Apology: for while in the first member of the trilogy we have Socrates' *Apologia pro vita sua*, the other two set before us his *Apologia pro morte sua:* in the Crito we have the citizen's justification for remaining to die, in the Phaedo the philosopher's, the hope of immortality. But on a closer examination we shall see that our dialogue is rather an epilogue to the Apology than a prologue to the Phaedo. There is little in the doctrine of the two first dialogues that travels beyond the standpoint of the historical Socrates, whereas in the purely philosophical sections of the Phaedo, Socrates speaks for Plato rather than for himself. And in the second place, we are introduced in the Crito to an elaborate refutation of the political prejudice against Socrates which lent such fatal force to the indictment[1], a prejudice touched upon, it is true, in the Apology[2], but for the first time thoroughly exposed and rebutted in our dialogue. So far from being the enemy of his country and the corrupter of his fellow-citizens, the Crito sets before us Socrates as the only true patriot, faithful to his country and her laws even at a moment when average Athenian morality as interpreted by the mouth of Crito pronounced it to be not only ex-

[1] See my Introduction to the Apology, pp. xxiv—xxv.
[2] Chapters xix—xxii.

cusable but his imperative duty to break the laws and save his life[1]. The structure of the dialogue is admirably adapted for the purpose of exhibiting the patriotism of Socrates, and reveals throughout a close analogy to the actual circumstances of Socrates' trial, defence and condemnation. As the correct apprehension of this analogy will bring still more clearly into view the real scope and meaning of the Crito, I will endeavour to trace it in detail: the subject-matter of our dialogue will be considered later.

In the trial of Socrates, there were three parties concerned—the prosecution, represented by Meletus and his associates, Socrates himself as the defendant, and the judges. The charge was virtually one of High Treason : Socrates, it was alleged, had been unfaithful to his country by endeavouring to demoralise her youth and refusing to recognise her gods. A verdict of guilty was returned and Socrates condemned to death: this much the Apology gives us. In the Crito, as it appears to me, the semblance of a trial is still preserved, under the mask of dialogue. This time Socrates is judge, Crito prosecutor, the State prisoner at the bar. The charge is wrong-doing (ἀδικεῖν): the verdict one of acquittal. I see frequent indications of such a juridical structure throughout the Crito, such as the personification of the Laws, the use of ἀπολλύναι νόμους as a figurative expression for breaking the laws (50 A, 50 D, 51 A, 54 C), perhaps also the use of εἰσηγεῖσθαι in 48 A (οὐκ ὀρθῶς εἰσηγεῖ, εἰσηγούμενος τῆς τῶν πολλῶν δόξης δεῖν ἡμᾶς φροντίζειν περὶ τῶν δικαίων καὶ καλῶν καὶ ἀγαθῶν καὶ τῶν ἐναντίων), and in particular the words of Socrates in 50 B,

[1] See Crito, Chapter v.

just after the Laws have been brought upon the stage: πολλὰ γὰρ ἄν τις ἔχοι, ἄλλως τε καὶ ῥήτωρ, εἰπεῖν ὑπὲρ τούτου τοῦ νόμου ἀπολλυμένου ὃς τὰς δίκας τὰς δικασθείσας προστάττει κυρίας εἶναι[1]. The framework upon which the Crito hangs is hidden throughout the two opening chapters by the dramatic setting of the dialogue, nor does it emerge into view for some time, owing to the peculiar form which Crito's speech against the State of necessity assumed: partly for artistic reasons, and partly no doubt in order to conform to historical truth, Plato felt bound to make Crito arraign the State indirectly rather than directly—by means of earnest entreaties addressed to Socrates urging him to effect an illegal escape. It is not till we reach the sixth Chapter, in which Socrates begins to expound and emphasize the principle upon which the verdict ought to hinge, that the essentially legal structure of the dialogue first comes clearly before our eyes. Socrates the judge lays down the higher and unwritten law by which the State is to be judged. οὔτε ἄρα ἀνταδικεῖν δεῖ οὔτε κακῶς ποιεῖν οὐδένα ἀνθρώπων, οὐδ' ἂν ὁτιοῦν πάσχῃ ὑπ' αὐτῶν (49 C). The State is next heard in her own defence: she pleads that her very existence is endangered (XI), that Socrates above all Athenians owes her even more than filial obedience and regard (XIII—XIV), finally, after a brief reply to the arguments of Crito (XV), she concludes by hold-ing out to Socrates a prospect of rewards in the

---

[1] Cron's remark on this passage is true, but not (I think) the whole truth: "Dabei wird man an die Sitte zu Athen erinnert, dass, wenn es sich um Abschaffung eines Gesetzes handelte, dieses durch erwählte Anwälte (συνήγοροι) vertheidigt wurde.'

other world, at the same time reiterating her own innocence: ἠδικημένος ἄπει, ἐὰν ἀπίῃς, οὐχ ὑφ᾽ ἡμῶν, ἀλλὰ ὑπὸ ἀνθρώπων (54 Β). Socrates then pronounces verdict of acquittal: ἔα τοίνυν, ὦ Κρίτων, καὶ πράττωμεν ταύτῃ, ἐπειδὴ ταύτῃ ὁ θεὸς ὑφηγεῖται.

Enough has now been said to establish what is I think a clear analogy between the structure of our dialogue and the circumstances of Socrates' trial: but in order to obtain an accurate comprehension of the meaning of the verdict delivered by Socrates, it is necessary to inquire somewhat more particularly into the position assigned to Crito and to the Laws. Crito is not merely the friend of Socrates, pleading with passionate earnestness against the sacrifice of the associate whom he held so dear: he is also the mouthpiece of Athenian public opinion. This is clearly implied in the arguments by which he endeavours to induce Socrates to make his escape: "many men," he says in 44 Β, "who do not know you and me well, will think me guilty of neglect, because I might have saved you, if I had been willing to spend money": and again in 45 Ε, "I for my part feel ashamed for you and for us who are your friends. It will be thought that the whole of this thing which has befallen you is due to our cowardice, I mean your appearance in court when you need not have appeared, the process itself, and last of all, the crowning absurdity of the whole transaction, that you should be thought to have given us the slip through a sort of cowardice and unmanliness upon our part, because we did not save you and you did not save yourself, when it was possible and practicable for you to do so, if we had been good for anything at all." Had Socrates complied with the invitation of his friend, not only would no Athenian have condemned

him, but to the mass of his countrymen his conduct
would have appeared not only natural, but perfectly
just: the ties of friendship were stronger in their esti-
mation than those of patriotism. Speaking of the
reproaches which he would have to endure for leaving
Socrates to die, Crito asks in 44 C: "what character
could be more dishonourable than the character of
preferring one's money to one's friends? The people
will never believe that it was you who refused to
escape, and we who were anxious to save you." The
concluding part of Crito's appeal is even more emphatic: "And besides, Socrates, I think you are trying to
do what is *wrong*, betraying yourself, when you might
be saved (45 C)." Crito is throughout the represen-
tative of average Athenian morality, and from the
fact that he nowhere recognises the paramount duty
which both Socrates and he as surety for his friend
owed to the State, we can see how lightly the yoke
of patriotism pressed upon an age that produced a
Theramenes and an Alcibiades.

Let us now examine the part played by the Laws in
the dialogue. It is easy to go wrong here: for that
which is acquitted by Socrates is not the verdict or
sentence which the unjust judges had pronounced
against him: Socrates indeed declares again and again
throughout the dialogue that his condemnation was
flagrantly unjust. Nor yet is it strictly speaking the
constitution of Athens in particular, for Socrates was
far from viewing democracy with an altogether favour-
able eye: but what really stands arraigned before him

---

[1] It has been supposed that Crito stood surety not after, but
before the trial. The language of Phaedo 115 D is against such a
view, and it should be remembered that surety might well be
needed against the escape of a prisoner whose friends had access
to the prison.

is the State in the abstract as opposed to the Individual—in other words the principle that alone renders
possible the existence of any kind of State, aristocracy
no less than democracy, the νόμος ὃς προστάττει τὰς
δίκας τὰς δικασθείσας κυρίας εἶναι (50 B).

We are now in a position to comprehend the full
meaning of Socrates' decision. His acquittal of the
State is at once a condemnation of his judges and a
counter-accusation of High Treason against the people
themselves. For if the State was innocent, the guilt
rested with the judges, who had misinterpreted the
law : and the postponement of public interests to the
apparent advantage of the individual, which forms the
very pith and marrow of Crito's appeal, is shewn to be
just as treasonable as Socrates himself was patriotic.

Up to this point we have been concerned chiefly
with the form of the dialogue : it remains to consider
the doctrine. We shall find that both in respect of
ethical and political teaching the Crito remains true
to the creed of the historical Socrates. This is exactly
what we should expect beforehand, if the real purpose
of Plato, as I have endeavoured to shew, was to hurl
back the charge of High Treason from the Socrates of
history upon the Athenians at large.

We note first of all the peculiarly Socratic method
which is employed throughout the inquiry. The entire
dialogue is but an illustration of the precept which is
enunciated in 46 B: ἐγὼ οὐ μόνον νῦν, ἀλλὰ καὶ ἀεὶ τοιοῦτος, οἷος τῶν ἐμῶν μηδενὶ ἄλλῳ πείθεσθαι ἢ τῷ λόγῳ,
ὃς ἄν μοι λογιζομένῳ βέλτιστος φαίνηται[1]. Here
the λόγος is μηδενὶ τρόπῳ ἀδικητέον εἶναι: it forms so
to speak the major premise of Socrates' practical syllo-
gism, of which the minor is established by the plead-

ing of the Laws (50 A foll.). The historical accuracy
of our dialogue is apparent in its ethical doctrine no
less than in its method. We seem to hear the voice
of Socrates when we read that only the wise man's
judgment is deserving of regard (47 A), and still more
when we find this statement backed up by the familiar
illustrations from the arts (47 B foll.): nor is the conception of wickedness as a disease of the soul, and
the preference of soul over body (47 E foll.), out of
harmony with Socrates' teaching. Equally Socratic is
the sentiment in 48 B: οὐ τὸ ζῆν περὶ πλείστου ποιητέον,
ἀλλὰ τὸ εὖ ζῆν: and the refusal in 49 E to permit any
divergence between theory and practice is only the
οὐδεὶς ἑκὼν ἁμαρτάνει stripped of its paradox. I think
also that Socrates would have willingly accepted the
fundamental λόγος of the dialogue—μηδενὶ τρόπῳ ἀδικητέον εἶναι—even if he never actually so expressed
himself. The objections raised by Zeller and many
editors, on the ground of passages in Xenophon and
Aristotle[1], seem to be directed rather against the apparent altruism of such a doctrine than at the doctrine
itself. But in the mouth of Socrates the sentiment,
so far from being altruistic, was dictated by conscious
egoism. He refrained from doing wrong, not out of
regard for others, but because of its effect upon his
own soul: for just in proportion as the value of our

---

[1] In Mem. II. 6. 35 all that Socrates says is that if Crito-
bulus believes that virtue in a man is νικᾶν τοὺς μὲν φίλους εὖ
ποιοῦντα, τοὺς δὲ ἐχθροὺς κακῶς, he will not find it hard to make
friends. Mem. III. 9. 8 proves nothing either way. In Aristotle Rhet. II. 23, p. 1398ᵃ 24 (Σωκράτης οὐκ ἔφη βαδίζειν ὡς
Ἀρχέλαον· ὕβριν γὰρ εἶναι ἔφη τὸ μὴ δύνασθαι ἀμύνασθαι, ὥσπερ
καὶ κακῶς) it seems to me that Socrates is only making use of a
popular definition of ὕβρις to illustrate his own.

souls exceeds that of our bodies[1], is the supreme
importance of keeping them healthy and free from
stain, if we would consult our own individual interests.
<u>Rightly understood, this thorough-going vindication
of virtuous conduct even under the extremest provo-
cation</u> is altogether in harmony with a creed which
<u>regarded soul as the true self, and self-knowledge
and self-development as the end of life.</u>

The political teaching of the Crito faithfully represents the opinions held by Socrates and establishes
his right to the title of patriot, in contrast to his fellow-
countrymen. Whether we regard the decision itself,
or the grounds by which it is enforced, the whole
political bearing of the dialogue may be summed up
in the words which Xenophon puts into the mouth of
Socrates: φημὶ γὰρ ἐγὼ τὸ νόμιμον δίκαιον εἶναι (Mem.
IV. 4. 12). To break the laws is to strike at the root
of all society (50 A): it is not merely a breach of con-
tract (51 E), it is State-murder, a crime worse than
matricide (50 B, 51 A foll.), because our country is far
more to us than a mother. What an emphatic assertion of the old Greek theory of life is here! The very
man whose daily work it was to preach *self*-study and
self-knowledge proclaims that we should live for the
State rather than for ourselves. Nor if we view the
question rightly is there any contradiction. Socrates
refused to separate the βίος πρακτικός from the βίος
θεωρητικός; he claimed to be a political as well as a
moral reformer: οἶμαι μετ᾽ ὀλίγων Ἀθηναίων, he says
in the Gorgias, ἵνα μὴ εἴπω μόνος, ἐπιχειρεῖν τῇ ὡς ἀλη-

---

[1] See Mem. IV. 3. 14 ἀλλὰ μὴν καὶ ἀνθρώπου γε ψυχή, ἢ εἴπερ
τι καὶ ἄλλο τῶν ἀνθρωπίνων τοῦ θείου μετέχει and compare Crito
47 E—48 A.

θῶς πολιτικῇ τέχνῃ καὶ πράττειν τὰ πολιτικὰ μόνος τῶν νῦν (521 E). He exhorted the Athenians ἀφ' ἑστίας ἄρχεσθαι καθαίρειν τὴν πόλιν—to reform the State by reforming themselves: and, conversely, he believed that the full development of the individual could only be attained in the service of the State. The only possible life as it appeared to Socrates was the life of a citizen. He condemned the increasing divergence between public and private interests in his day, and traced to this among other causes the decline of Athenian prosperity (Mem. III. 5. 21).

It may appear strange that a man so prone to doubt and inquiry should have hesitated to call in question the authority of the laws: but the fact is undeniable. Socrates would have agreed with the remark of Cleon in Thucydides (III. 37. 4) οἱ μὲν γὰρ τῶν τε νόμων σοφώτεροι βούλονται φαίνεσθαι—καὶ ἐκ τοῦ τοιούτου τὰ πολλὰ σφάλλουσι τὰς πόλεις. His whole life was distinguished by absolute fidelity to the laws of his country: he had upheld them against the fury of the people and the tyranny of the thirty: and now he consents to death rather than break them. It was for their strict subordination to law and authority that Socrates entertained so warm an admiration for Sparta and Crete: and the same feeling underlies the praise which he bestows in Xenophon upon the Athens of the past (Mem. III. 5). The generation before his birth appeared to him a kind of golden age, when the State flourished and the citizens were happy under the old unreflecting morality, where no right was known but that of law. The limitation of Socrates' genius appears here. Had he carried out his principles to their fullest logical development, he would not have shrunk from submitting to the test of his dialectic the whole question of the validity and authority of law, as a condition of the stability of social life : but to him it is almost an axiom that the law should be obeyed. The fact is that Socrates' rationalism was only half-complete. If reason presided over one hemisphere, μαντική appeared to him to rule the other[1]. It was reserved for Plato to dethrone μαντική and make νοῦς the sole monarch of the world[2]. But in Socrates' way of thinking, the Laws derive their validity from God, and have no need of human reason to establish it : they are of the same family with the Laws in the Unseen World, and he who offends against the one is held guilty by the other : ἡμεῖς τέ σοι χαλεπανοῦμεν ζῶντι, καὶ ἐκεῖ οἱ ἡμέτεροι ἀδελφοὶ οἱ ἐν Ἅιδου νόμοι οὐκ εὐμενῶς σε ὑποδέξονται, εἰδότες ὅτι καὶ ἡμᾶς ἐπεχείρησας ἀπολέσαι τὸ σὸν μέρος (54 C)[3].

The Crito therefore presents us with what is upon the whole a faithful picture of Socrates both as a man and as a teacher. Only in two respects does it appear to travel beyond the views which may with certainty be ascribed to him. While still in the vigour of life and possessed with the ardour of his mission, Socrates on no occasion expressed himself so despairingly about his country as we should infer

---

[1] See this admirably worked out in Nohle's "Die Statslehre Platos in ihrer geschichtlichen Entwicklung" (Jena, 1880), pp. 10—13.

[2] In Politicus 209 C priests and soothsayers are placed on the same level with slaves, artisans and merchants.

[3] See also Xen. Mem. IV. 4. 25 καὶ τοῖς θεοῖς ἄρα, ὦ Ἱππία, τὸ αὐτὸ δίκαιόν τε καὶ νόμιμον εἶναι ἀρέσκει.

from various passages in the Crito[1]: on the contrary
he thought the reformation of Athens quite within the
range of practical politics (Xen. Mem. III. 5). Nor
would he have spoken of a future life so confidently as
the Laws with his approval speak towards the close of
the dialogue. But even here we must allow something
for the influence which the imminent prospect of death
might exert even upon the ardent spirit and sternly
logical mind of a Socrates. On the whole I think it
probable that his unjust condemnation may have led
him to despair, not so much of Athens, as of the
Athenians : but I cannot bring myself to believe that
he could ever have dogmatically asserted or approved
of the doctrine of immortality. Plato seems to be
responsible for that.

In conclusion, let us endeavour to sum up the
reasons which induced Socrates to remain and die.
First and foremost, we may put the influence of his
'divine sign.' Although this is nowhere expressly
mentioned in the Crito, yet there seems to be an
allusion to it in the words with which the dialogue
concludes—πράττωμεν ταύτῃ, ἐπειδὴ ταύτῃ ὁ θεὸς ὑφηγεῖται. The very pleading of the Laws is but the
voice of the divine sign made articulate : see my note
upon 54 D καὶ ἐν ἐμοὶ αὕτη ἡ ἠχὴ τούτων τῶν λόγων
βομβεῖ καὶ ποιεῖ μὴ δύνασθαι τῶν ἄλλων ἀκούειν. The
rejection too of Crito's offer was the best possible
refutation of the charge of treason, as it revealed
Socrates in the light of a true patriot in the midst

---

[1] 44 D, 48 C and especially 49 D οἶδα γὰρ ὅτι ὀλίγοις τισὶ
ταῦτα καὶ δοκεῖ καὶ δόξει. οἷς οὖν οὕτω δέδοκται καὶ οἷς μή, τούτοις
οὐκ ἔστι κοινὴ βουλή, ἀλλ' ἀνάγκη τούτους ἀλλήλων καταφρονεῖν,
ὁρῶντας τὰ ἀλλήλων βουλεύματα.

of men, with whom private and personal interests weighed more than regard for their country and her laws. Nor must we forget, in the third place, that Socrates was now old, and had finished his mission: it was hardly possible to find a more opportune moment for dying. The death of Socrates was the best thing that could happen for his fame and influence: it was well worth while to die, if only for the sake of the impulse which his death imparted to the greatest of his pupils.

ΚΡΙΤΩΝ.

[ἢ περὶ πρακτέογ. ἠθικόc.]

————

ΤΑ ΤΟΥ ΔΙΑΛΟΓΟΥ ΠΡΟΣΩΠΑ

ΣΩΚΡΑΤΗΣ, ΚΡΙΤΩΝ.

I. ΣΩ. Τί τηνικάδε ἀφῖξαι, ὦ Κρίτων; ἢ οὐ πρῷ ἔτι ἐστίν;

КР. Πάνυ μὲν οὖν.

ΣΩ. Πηνίκα μάλιστα;

ΚΡ. Ὄρθρος βαθύς.

Crito visits Socrates in prison. 'To-day, Socrates, the ship will return from Delos, and to-morrow you must 5 die.'

ΣΩ. Θαυμάζω, ὅπως ἠθέλησέ σοι ὁ τοῦ δεσμωτηρίου φύλαξ ὑπακοῦσαι.

ΚΡ. Ξυνήθης ἤδη μοί ἐστιν, ὦ Σώκρατες, διὰ τὸ πολλάκις δεῦρο φοιτᾶν, καί τι καὶ εὐηργέτηται ὑπ' ἐμοῦ.

ΣΩ. Ἄρτι δὲ ἥκεις ἢ πάλαι;

ΚΡ. Ἐπιεικῶς πάλαι.

B ΣΩ. Εἶτα πῶς οὐκ εὐθὺς ἐπήγειράς με, ἀλλὰ σιγῇ παρακάθησαι;

ΚΡ. Οὐ μὰ τὸν Δία, ὦ Σώκρατες· οὐδ' ἂν αὐτὸς 15 ἤθελον ἐν τοσαύτῃ τε ἀγρυπνίᾳ καὶ λύπῃ εἶναι.

ἀλλὰ καὶ σοῦ πάλαι θαυμάζω, αἰσθανόμενος, ὡς ἡδέως
καθεύδεις· καὶ ἐπίτηδές σε οὐκ ἤγειρον, ἵνα ὡς
ἥδιστα διάγῃς. καὶ πολλάκις μὲν δή σε καὶ πρότε-
20 ρον ἐν παντὶ τῷ βίῳ ηὐδαιμόνισα τοῦ τρόπου, πολὺ
δὲ μάλιστα ἐν τῇ νῦν παρεστώσῃ ξυμφορᾷ, ὡς ῥᾳδίως
αὐτὴν καὶ πρᾴως φέρεις.

ΣΩ. Καὶ γὰρ ἄν, ὦ Κρίτων, πλημμελὲς εἴη ἀγανακτεῖν τηλικοῦτον ὄντα, εἰ δεῖ ἤδη τελευτᾶν.

25 ΚΡ. Καὶ ἄλλοι, ὦ Σώκρατες, τηλικοῦτοι ἐν τοι- C
αύταις ξυμφοραῖς ἁλίσκονται, ἀλλ᾽ οὐδὲν αὐτοὺς ἐπιλύεται ἡ ἡλικία τὸ μὴ οὐχὶ ἀγανακτεῖν τῇ παρούσῃ
τύχῃ.

ΣΩ. Ἔστι ταῦτα. ἀλλὰ τί δὴ οὕτω πρῷ
30 ἀφῖξαι;

ΚΡ. Ἀγγελίαν, ὦ Σώκρατες, φέρων χαλεπήν, οὐ
σοί, ὡς ἐμοὶ φαίνεται, ἀλλ᾽ ἐμοὶ καὶ τοῖς σοῖς ἐπιτη-
δείοις πᾶσιν καὶ χαλεπὴν καὶ βαρεῖαν, ἣν ἐγώ, ὡς
ἐμοὶ δοκῶ, ἐν τοῖς βαρύτατ᾽ ἂν ἐνέγκαιμι.

35 ΣΩ. Τίνα ταύτην; ἢ τὸ πλοῖον ἀφῖκται ἐκ
Δήλου, οὗ δεῖ ἀφικομένου τεθνάναι με;

ΚΡ. Οὔ τοι δὴ ἀφῖκται, ἀλλὰ δοκεῖ μέν μοι ἥξειν D
τήμερον ἐξ ὧν ἀπαγγέλλουσιν ἥκοντές τινες ἀπὸ
Σουνίου καὶ καταλιπόντες ἐκεῖ αὐτό. δῆλον οὖν ἐκ
40 τούτων τῶν ἀγγέλων, ὅτι ἥξει τήμερον, καὶ ἀνάγκη δὴ
εἰς αὔριον ἔσται, ὦ Σώκρατες, τὸν βίον σε τελευτᾶν.

II. ΣΩ. Ἀλλ᾽, ὦ Κρίτων, τύχῃ ἀγαθῇ. εἰ
ταύτῃ τοῖς θεοῖς φίλον, ταύτῃ ἔστω. οὐ

'The ship will
arrive to morrow.
A vision has told
me that I shall
live two days.'

μέντοι οἶμαι ἥξειν αὐτὸ τήμερον.

ΚΡ. | Πόθεν τοῦτο τεκμαίρει;
44
5 ΣΩ. Ἐγώ σοι ἐρῶ. τῇ γάρ που
ὑστεραίᾳ δεῖ με ἀποθνῄσκειν ἢ ᾗ ἂν ἔλθῃ τὸ πλοῖον.

ΚΡ.　Φασί γέ τοι δὴ οἱ τούτων κύριοι.

ΣΩ.　Οὐ τοίνυν τῆς ἐπιούσης ἡμέρας οἶμαι αὐτὸ
ἥξειν, ἀλλὰ τῆς ἑτέρας. τεκμαίρομαι δὲ ἔκ τινος
ἐνυπνίου, ὃ ἑώρακα ὀλίγον πρότερον ταύτης τῆς 10
νυκτός. καὶ κινδυνεύεις ἐν καιρῷ τινι οὐκ ἐγείραί
με.

ΚΡ.　Ἦν δὲ δὴ τί τὸ ἐνύπνιον;

ΣΩ.　Ἐδόκει τίς μοι γυνὴ προσελθοῦσα καλὴ
Β καὶ εὐειδής, λευκὰ ἱμάτια ἔχουσα, καλέσαι με καὶ 15
εἰπεῖν· ὦ Σώκρατες, ἤματί κεν τριτάτῳ Φθίην
ἐρίβωλον ἵκοιο.

ΚΡ.　Ἄτοπον τὸ ἐνύπνιον, ὦ Σώκρατες.

ΣΩ.　Ἐναργὲς μὲν οὖν, ὥς γέ μοι δοκεῖ, ὦ
Κρίτων.　　　　　　　　　　　　　　　　　　20

III.　ΚΡ.　Λίαν γε, ὡς ἔοικεν. ἀλλ’, ὦ δαιμόνιε
Σώκρατες, ἔτι καὶ νῦν ἐμοὶ πείθου καὶ
σώθητι· ὡς ἐμοί, ἐὰν σὺ ἀποθάνῃς, οὐ
μία ξυμφορά ἐστιν, ἀλλὰ χωρὶς μὲν σοῦ
ἐστερῆσθαι, τοιούτου ἐπιτηδείου, οἷον ἐγὼ
οὐδένα μή ποτε εὑρήσω, ἔτι δὲ καὶ
πολλοῖς δόξω, οἳ ἐμὲ καὶ σὲ μὴ σαφῶς ἴσασιν, ὡς οἷός
C τ’ ὢν σε σώζειν, εἰ ἤθελον ἀναλίσκειν χρήματα, ἀμελῆσαι. καί τοι τίς ἂν αἰσχίων εἴη ταύτης δόξα ἢ
δοκεῖν χρήματα περὶ πλείονος ποιεῖσθαι ἢ φίλους; 10
οὐ γὰρ πείσονται οἱ πολλοί, ὡς σὺ αὐτὸς οὐκ ἠθέλη-
σας ἀπιέναι ἐνθένδε ἡμῶν προθυμουμένων.

ΣΩ.　Ἀλλὰ τί ἡμῖν, ὦ μακάριε Κρίτων, οὕτω τῆς
τῶν πολλῶν δόξης μέλει; οἱ γὰρ ἐπιεικέστατοι, ὧν
μᾶλλον ἄξιον φροντίζειν, ἡγήσονται αὐτὰ οὕτω πε- 15
πρᾶχθαι, ὥσπερ ἂν πραχθῇ.

D　ΚΡ.　Ἀλλ’ ὁρᾷς δὴ ὅτι ἀνάγκη, ὦ Σώκρατες, καὶ

'For my sake, Socrates, I en-
treat you to make
your escape from
prison. Think
what men will 5
say of me.

τῆς τῶν πολλῶν δόξης μέλειν. αὐτὰ δὲ δῆλα τὰ
παρόντα νυνί, ὅτι οἷοί τ᾽ εἰσὶν οἱ πολλοὶ οὐ τὰ
20 σμικρότατα τῶν κακῶν ἐξεργάζεσθαι, ἀλλὰ τὰ μέγιστα σχεδόν, ἐάν τις ἐν αὐτοῖς διαβεβλημένος ᾖ.

ΣΩ. Εἰ γὰρ ὤφελον, ὦ Κρίτων, οἷοί τ᾽ εἶναι οἱ
πολλοὶ τὰ μέγιστα κακὰ ἐργάζεσθαι, ἵνα οἷοί τ᾽ ἦσαν
καὶ ἀγαθὰ τὰ μέγιστα, καὶ καλῶς ἂν εἶχεν· νῦν δὲ
25 οὐδέτερα οἷοί τε· οὔτε γὰρ φρόνιμον οὔτε ἄφρονα
δυνατοὶ ποιῆσαι, ποιοῦσι δὲ τοῦτο ὅ τι ἂν τύχωσι.

IV. ΚΡ. Ταῦτα μὲν δὴ οὕτως ἐχέτω· τάδε δέ, E
ὦ Σώκρατες, εἰπέ μοι. ἆρά γε μὴ ἐμοῦ
προμηθεῖ καὶ τῶν ἄλλων ἐπιτηδείων, μή,
ἐὰν σὺ ἐνθένδε ἐξέλθῃς, οἱ συκοφάνται
5   ἡμῖν πράγματα παρέχωσιν ὡς σὲ ἐνθένδε
ἐκκλέψασιν, καὶ ἀναγκασθῶμεν ἢ καὶ πᾶσαν τὴν
οὐσίαν ἀποβαλεῖν ἢ συχνὰ χρήματα, ἢ καὶ ἄλλο τι
πρὸς τούτοις παθεῖν; εἰ γάρ τι τοιοῦτον | φοβεῖ, ἔασον 4.
αὐτὸ χαίρειν· ἡμεῖς γάρ που δίκαιοί ἐσμεν σώσαντές
10 σε κινδυνεύειν τοῦτον τὸν κίνδυνον καί, ἐὰν δέῃ, ἔτι
τούτου μεῖζω. ἀλλ᾽ ἐμοὶ πείθου καὶ μὴ ἄλλως ποίει.

ΣΩ. Καὶ ταῦτα προμηθοῦμαι, ὦ Κρίτων, καὶ
ἄλλα πολλά.

ΚΡ. Μήτε τοίνυν ταῦτα φοβοῦ· καὶ γὰρ οὐδὲ
15 πολὺ τἀργύριόν ἐστιν, ὃ θέλουσι λαβόντες τινὲς
σῶσαί σε καὶ ἐξαγαγεῖν ἐνθένδε. ἔπειτα οὐχ ὁρᾷς
τούτους τοὺς συκοφάντας ὡς εὐτελεῖς, καὶ οὐδὲν ἂν
δέοι ἐπ᾽ αὐτοὺς πολλοῦ ἀργυρίου; σοὶ δὲ ὑπάρχει μὲν
τὰ ἐμὰ χρήματα, ὡς ἐγὼ οἶμαι, ἱκανά· ἔπειτα καὶ εἴ τι B
20 ἐμοῦ κηδόμενος οὐκ οἴει δεῖν ἀναλίσκειν τἀμά, ξένοι
οὗτοι ἐνθάδε ἕτοιμοι ἀναλίσκειν· εἰς δὲ καὶ κεκόμικεν
ἐπ᾽ αὐτὸ τοῦτο ἀργύριον ἱκανόν, Σιμμίας ὁ Θηβαῖος·

ἕτοιμος δὲ καὶ Κέβης καὶ ἄλλοι πολλοὶ πάνυ. ὥστε,
ὅπερ λέγω, μήτε ταῦτα φοβούμενος ἀποκάμῃς σαυτὸν
σῶσαι, μήτε, ὃ ἔλεγες ἐν τῷ δικαστηρίῳ, δυσχερές σοι 25
γενέσθω, ὅτι οὐκ ἂν ἔχοις ἐξελθὼν ὅ τι χρῷο σαυτῷ·
πολλαχοῦ μὲν γὰρ καὶ ἄλλοσε, ὅποι ἂν ἀφίκῃ, ἀγα-
C πήσουσί σε· ἐὰν δὲ βούλῃ εἰς Θετταλίαν ἰέναι, εἰσὶν
ἐμοὶ ἐκεῖ ξένοι, οἵ σε περὶ πολλοῦ ποιήσονται καὶ
ἀσφάλειάν σοι παρέξονται, ὥστε σε μηδένα λυπεῖν 30
τῶν κατὰ Θετταλίαν.

V. Ἔτι δέ, ὦ Σώκρατες, οὐδὲ δίκαιόν μοι δοκεῖς
ἐπιχειρεῖν πρᾶγμα, σαυτὸν προδοῦναι,
ἐξὸν σωθῆναι· καὶ τοιαῦτα σπεύδεις περὶ
σαυτὸν γενέσθαι, ἅπερ ἂν καὶ οἱ ἐχθροί
σου σπεύσαιέν τε καὶ ἔσπευσαν σὲ διαφθεῖραι βουλόμενοι. πρὸς δὲ τούτοις καὶ
τοὺς υἱεῖς τοὺς σαυτοῦ ἔμοιγε δοκεῖς προ-
D διδόναι, οὕς σοι ἐξὸν καὶ ἐκθρέψαι καὶ
ἐκπαιδεῦσαι οἰχήσει καταλιπών, καὶ τὸ σὸν μέρος, ὅ
τι ἂν τύχωσι, τοῦτο πράξουσιν· τεύξονται δέ, ὡς τὸ 10
εἰκός, τοιούτων οἷάπερ εἴωθεν γίγνεσθαι ἐν ταῖς ὀρφανίαις περὶ τοὺς ὀρφανούς. ἢ γὰρ οὐ χρὴ ποιεῖσθαι
παῖδας, ἢ ξυνδιαταλαιπωρεῖν καὶ τρέφοντα καὶ παι-
δεύοντα· σὺ δέ μοι δοκεῖς τὰ ῥαθυμότατα αἱρεῖσθαι·
χρὴ δέ, ἅπερ ἂν ἀνὴρ ἀγαθὸς καὶ ἀνδρεῖος ἕλοιτο, 15
ταῦτα αἱρεῖσθαι, φάσκοντά γε δὴ ἀρετῆς διὰ παντὸς
τοῦ βίου ἐπιμελεῖσθαι· ὡς ἔγωγε καὶ ὑπὲρ σοῦ καὶ
E ὑπὲρ ἡμῶν τῶν σῶν ἐπιτηδείων αἰσχύνομαι, μὴ δόξῃ
ἅπαν τὸ πρᾶγμα τὸ περὶ σὲ ἀνανδρίᾳ τινὶ τῇ
ἡμετέρᾳ πεπρᾶχθαι, καὶ ἡ εἴσοδος τῆς δίκης εἰς τὸ 20
δικαστήριον ὡς εἰσῆλθες ἐξὸν μὴ εἰσελθεῖν, καὶ αὐτὸς
ὁ ἀγὼν τῆς δίκης ὡς ἐγένετο, καὶ τὸ τελευταῖον δὴ

Besides it is
wrong, even cow-
ardly, to die when
you might live.
Think of your
children and your 5
friends: we shall
be branded as
cowards for our
share in this whole
matter.'

τουτί, ὥσπερ κατάγελως τῆς πράξεως, κακίᾳ τινὶ καὶ
ἀνανδρίᾳ τῇ ἡμετέρᾳ διαπεφευγέναι | ἡμᾶς δοκεῖν, οἵ- 46
25 τινές σε οὐχὶ ἐσώσαμεν οὐδὲ σὺ σαυτόν, οἷόν τε ὂν
καὶ δυνατόν, εἴ τι καὶ μικρὸν ἡμῶν ὄφελος ἦν. ταῦτα
οὖν, ὦ Σώκρατες, ὅρα μὴ ἅμα τῷ κακῷ καὶ αἰσχρὰ ᾖ
σοί τε καὶ ἡμῖν. ἀλλὰ βουλεύου, μᾶλλον δὲ οὐδὲ
βουλεύεσθαι ἔτι ὥρα, ἀλλὰ βεβουλεῦσθαι. μία δὲ
30 βουλή· τῆς γὰρ ἐπιούσης νυκτὸς πάντα ταῦτα δεῖ
πεπρᾶχθαι. εἰ δ' ἔτι περιμενοῦμεν, ἀδύνατον καὶ
οὐκέτι οἷόν τε. ἀλλὰ παντὶ τρόπῳ, ὦ Σώκρατες,
πείθου μοι καὶ μηδαμῶς ἄλλως ποίει.

VI. ΣΩ. Ὦ φίλε Κρίτων, ἡ προθυμία σου B
πολλοῦ ἀξία, εἰ μετά τινος ὀρθότητος εἴη·
εἰ δὲ μή, ὅσῳ μείζων, τοσούτῳ χαλεπω-
τέρα. σκοπεῖσθαι οὖν χρὴ ἡμᾶς, εἴτε
5 ταῦτα πρακτέον εἴτε μή· ὡς ἐγὼ οὐ μόνον
νῦν, ἀλλὰ καὶ ἀεὶ τοιοῦτος, οἷος τῶν ἐμῶν μηδενὶ
ἄλλῳ πείθεσθαι ἢ τῷ λόγῳ, ὃς ἄν μοι λογιζομένῳ
βέλτιστος φαίνηται. τοὺς δὲ λόγους, οὓς ἐν τῷ ἔμπροσθεν ἔλεγον, οὐ δύναμαι νῦν ἐκβαλεῖν, ἐπειδή μοι
10 ἥδε ἡ τύχη γέγονεν, ἀλλὰ σχεδόν τι ὅμοιοι φαίνονταί
μοι, καὶ τοὺς αὐτοὺς πρεσβεύω καὶ τιμῶ, οὕσπερ καὶ C
πρότερον· ὧν ἐὰν μὴ βελτίω ἔχωμεν λέγειν ἐν τῷ
παρόντι, εὖ ἴσθι ὅτι οὐ μή σοι ξυγχωρήσω, οὐδ' ἂν
πλείω τῶν νῦν παρόντων ἢ τῶν πολλῶν δύναμις
15 ὥσπερ παῖδας ἡμᾶς μορμολύττηται, δεσμοὺς καὶ θανάτους ἐπιπέμπουσα καὶ χρημάτων ἀφαιρέσεις. πῶς
οὖν ἂν μετριώτατα σκοποίμεθα αὐτά; εἰ πρῶτον μὲν
τοῦτον τὸν λόγον ἀναλάβοιμεν, ὃν σὺ λέγεις περὶ τῶν
δοξῶν, πότερον καλῶς ἐλέγετο ἑκάστοτε ἢ οὔ, ὅτι ταῖς
20 μὲν δεῖ τῶν δοξῶν προσέχειν τὸν νοῦν, ταῖς δὲ οὔ· ἢ D

'Crito, the only
opinions worth
regarding are
those of the wise.
Is it not so?'
'Yes.'

πρὶν μὲν ἐμὲ δεῖν ἀποθνήσκειν καλῶς ἐλέγετο, νῦν δὲ
κατάδηλος ἄρα ἐγένετο, ὅτι ἄλλως [ἕνεκα λόγου] ἐλέγετο, ἦν δὲ παιδιὰ καὶ φλυαρία ὡς ἀληθῶς; ἐπιθυμῶ δ'
ἔγωγ' ἐπισκέψασθαι, ὦ Κρίτων, κοινῇ μετὰ σοῦ, εἴ τί
μοι ἀλλοιότερος φανεῖται, ἐπειδὴ ὧδε ἔχω, ἢ ὁ αὐτός, 25
καὶ ἐάσομεν χαίρειν ἢ πεισόμεθα αὐτῷ. ἐλέγετο δέ
πως, ὡς ἐγῷμαι, ἑκάστοτε ὧδε ὑπὸ τῶν οἰομένων τι
λέγειν, ὥσπερ νῦν δὴ ἐγὼ ἔλεγον, ὅτι τῶν δοξῶν, ἃς
οἱ ἄνθρωποι δοξάζουσιν, δέοι τὰς μὲν περὶ πολλοῦ
E ποιεῖσθαι, τὰς δὲ μή. τοῦτο πρὸς θεῶν, ὦ Κρίτων, 30
οὐ δοκεῖ καλῶς σοι λέγεσθαι; σὺ γάρ, ὅσα γε τἀν-
47 θρώπεια, ἐκτὸς εἶ τοῦ μέλλειν ἀποθνήσκειν | αὔριον,
καὶ οὐκ ἂν σὲ παρακρούοι ἡ παροῦσα ξυμφορά.
σκόπει δή· οὐχ ἱκανῶς δοκεῖ σοι λέγεσθαι, ὅτι οὐ
πάσας χρὴ τὰς δόξας τῶν ἀνθρώπων τιμᾶν, ἀλλὰ 35
τὰς μέν, τὰς δ' οὔ; τί φῄς; ταῦτα οὐχὶ καλῶς
λέγεται;

ΚΡ. Καλῶς.

ΣΩ. Οὐκοῦν τὰς μὲν χρηστὰς τιμᾶν, τὰς δὲ πο-
νηρὰς μή;
                                       40

ΚΡ. Ναί.

ΣΩ. Χρησταὶ δὲ οὐχ αἱ τῶν φρονίμων, πονηραὶ
δὲ αἱ τῶν ἀφρόνων;

ΚΡ. Πῶς δ' οὔ;

VII. ΣΩ. Φέρε δή, πῶς αὖ τὰ τοιαῦτα ἐλέγετο;
B γυμναζόμενος ἀνὴρ καὶ τοῦτο πράττων
πότερον παντὸς ἀνδρὸς ἐπαίνῳ καὶ ψόγῳ
τὸν νοῦν προσέχει, ἢ ἑνὸς μόνου ἐκείνου,
ὃς ἂν τυγχάνῃ ἰατρὸς ἢ παιδοτρίβης ὤν;

ΚΡ. Ἑνὸς μόνου.

ΣΩ. Οὐκοῦν φοβεῖσθαι χρὴ τοὺς

'As in gymnas-
tics, so in ques-
tions of right and
wrong: we should
regard, not the
opinions of the
many, but only 5
his who knows.
Otherwise that
within us which
is concerned with

right and wrong
will be destroyed:

ψόγους καὶ ἀσπάζεσθαι τοὺς ἐπαίνους
τοὺς τοῦ ἑνὸς ἐκείνου, ἀλλὰ μὴ τοὺς τῶν
10 πολλῶν.

ΚΡ.   Δῆλα δή.

ΣΩ.   Ταύτῃ ἄρα αὐτῷ πρακτέον καὶ γυμναστέον
καὶ ἐδεστέον γε καὶ ποτέον, ᾗ ἂν τῷ ἑνὶ δοκῇ τῷ
ἐπιστάτῃ καὶ ἐπαΐοντι, μᾶλλον ἢ ᾗ ξύμπασι τοῖς
15 ἄλλοις.

ΚΡ.   Ἔστι ταῦτα.

ΣΩ.   Εἶεν. ἀπειθήσας δὲ τῷ ἑνὶ καὶ ἀτιμάσας
αὐτοῦ τὴν δόξαν καὶ τοὺς ἐπαίνους, τιμήσας δὲ τοὺς C
τῶν πολλῶν λόγους καὶ μηδὲν ἐπαΐοντων, ἆρα οὐδὲν
20 κακὸν πείσεται;

ΚΡ.   Πῶς γὰρ οὔ;

ΣΩ.   Τί δ᾽ ἔστι τὸ κακὸν τοῦτο; καὶ ποῖ τείνει,
καὶ εἰς τί τῶν τοῦ ἀπειθοῦντος;

ΚΡ.   Δῆλον ὅτι εἰς τὸ σῶμα· τοῦτο γὰρ διόλλυσι.

25 ΣΩ.   Καλῶς λέγεις. οὐκοῦν καὶ τἆλλα, ὦ Κρίτων, οὕτως, ἵνα μὴ πάντα διΐωμεν, καὶ δὴ καὶ περὶ τῶν
δικαίων καὶ ἀδίκων καὶ αἰσχρῶν καὶ καλῶν καὶ ἀγαθῶν
καὶ κακῶν, περὶ ὧν νῦν ἡ βουλὴ ἡμῖν ἐστιν; πότερον D
τῇ τῶν πολλῶν δόξῃ δεῖ ἡμᾶς ἕπεσθαι καὶ φοβεῖσθαι
30 αὐτήν, ἢ τῇ τοῦ ἑνός, εἴ τίς ἐστιν ἐπαΐων, ὃν δεῖ καὶ
αἰσχύνεσθαι καὶ φοβεῖσθαι μᾶλλον ἢ ξύμπαντας τοὺς
ἄλλους; ᾧ εἰ μὴ ἀκολουθήσομεν, διαφθεροῦμεν ἐκεῖνο
καὶ λωβησόμεθα, ὃ τῷ μὲν δικαίῳ βέλτιον ἐγίγνετο,
τῷ δὲ ἀδίκῳ ἀπώλλυτο. ἢ οὐδέν ἐστι τοῦτο;

35 ΚΡ.   Οἶμαι ἔγωγε, ὦ Σώκρατες.

VIII.   ΣΩ.   Φέρε δή, ἐὰν τὸ ὑπὸ τοῦ ὑγιεινοῦ

and life would
then be intolera-
ble. It is true.

μὲν βέλτιον γιγνόμενον, ὑπὸ τοῦ νοσώδους δὲ διαφθειρόμενον διολέσωμεν πει-

θόμενοι μὴ τῇ τῶν ἐπαϊόντων δόξῃ, ἆρα
Ε βιωτὸν ἡμῖν ἐστιν διεφθαρμένου αὐτοῦ;
ἔστι δέ που τοῦτο τὸ σῶμα· ἢ οὐχί;

the many may put
us to death: but
life is not to be 5
bought at any
price.

ΚΡ. Ναί.

ΣΩ. Ἆρ' οὖν βιωτὸν ἡμῖν ἐστιν μετὰ μοχθηροῦ
καὶ διεφθαρμένου σώματος;

ΚΡ. Οὐδαμῶς.   10

ΣΩ. Ἀλλὰ μετ' ἐκείνου ἆρ' ἡμῖν βιωτὸν διεφθαρμένου, ᾧ τὸ ἄδικον μὲν λωβᾶται, τὸ δὲ δίκαιον
ὀνίνησιν; ἢ φαυλότερον ἡγούμεθα εἶναι τοῦ σώματος
ἐκεῖνο, ὅ τί ποτ' ἐστὶ τῶν | ἡμετέρων, περὶ ὃ ἥ τε
ἀδικία καὶ ἡ δικαιοσύνη ἐστίν;   15

ΚΡ. Οὐδαμῶς.

ΣΩ. Ἀλλὰ τιμιώτερον;

ΚΡ. Πολύ γε.

ΣΩ. Οὐκ ἄρα, ὦ βέλτιστε, πάνυ ἡμῖν οὕτω φρον-
τιστέον, τί ἐροῦσιν οἱ πολλοὶ ἡμᾶς, ἀλλ' ὅ τι ὁ ἐπαΐων 20
περὶ τῶν δικαίων καὶ ἀδίκων, ὁ εἷς, καὶ αὐτὴ ἡ ἀλήθεια. ὥστε πρῶτον μὲν ταύτῃ οὐκ ὀρθῶς εἰσηγεῖ,
εἰσηγούμενος τῆς τῶν πολλῶν δόξης δεῖν ἡμᾶς φροντίζειν περὶ τῶν δικαίων καὶ καλῶν καὶ ἀγαθῶν καὶ
τῶν ἐναντίων. ἀλλὰ μὲν δή, φαίη γ' ἄν τις, οἷοί τέ 25
εἰσιν ἡμᾶς οἱ πολλοὶ ἀποκτιννύναι.

ΚΡ. Δῆλα δὴ καὶ ταῦτα· φαίη γὰρ ἄν, ὦ Σώκρατες.

ΣΩ. Ἀληθῆ λέγεις. ἀλλ', ὦ θαυμάσιε, οὗτός
τε ὁ λόγος, ὃν διεληλύθαμεν, ἔμοιγε δοκεῖ ἔτι ὅμοιος 30
εἶναι καὶ πρότερον· καὶ τίνδε αὖ σκόπει, εἰ ἔτι μένει
ἡμῖν ἢ οὔ, ὅτι οὐ τὸ ζῆν περὶ πλείστου ποιητέον,
ἀλλὰ τὸ εὖ ζῆν.

ΚΡ. Ἀλλὰ μένει.

35 ΣΩ. Τὸ δὲ εὖ καὶ καλῶς καὶ δικαίως ὅτι ταὐτόν
ἐστιν, μένει ἢ οὐ μένει;

ΚΡ. Μένει.

IX. ΣΩ. Οὐκοῦν ἐκ τῶν ὁμολογουμένων τοῦτο
σκεπτέον, πότερον δίκαιον ἐμὲ ἐνθένδε

This is the question we have to ask—is it right or is it wrong for me to make my 5 escape? With the consequences to you or to my children or myself, we are not concerned.

πειρᾶσθαι ἐξιέναι μὴ ἀφιέντων Ἀθηναίων, ἢ οὐ δίκαιον· καὶ ἐὰν μὲν φαίνηται δίκαιον, πειρώμεθα, εἰ δὲ μή, ἐῶμεν.
ἃς δὲ σὺ λέγεις τὰς σκέψεις περί τε ἀναλώσεως χρημάτων καὶ δόξης καὶ παίδων
τροφῆς, μὴ ὡς ἀληθῶς ταῦτα, ὦ Κρίτων,
σκέμματα ᾖ τῶν ῥᾳδίως ἀποκτιννύντων καὶ ἀναβιω-
10 σκομένων γ᾽ ἄν, εἰ οἷοί τ᾽ ἦσαν, οὐδενὶ ξὺν νῷ, τούτων
τῶν πολλῶν. ἡμῖν δ᾽, ἐπειδὴ ὁ λόγος οὕτως αἱρεῖ,
μὴ οὐδὲν ἄλλο σκεπτέον ᾖ ἢ ὅπερ νῦν δὴ ἐλέγομεν,
πότερον δίκαια πράξομεν καὶ χρήματα τελοῦντες
τούτοις τοῖς ἐμὲ ἐνθένδε ἐξάξουσιν καὶ χάριτας, καὶ
15 αὐτοὶ ἐξάγοντές τε καὶ ἐξαγόμενοι, ἢ τῇ ἀληθείᾳ
ἀδικήσομεν πάντα ταῦτα ποιοῦντες· κἂν φαινώμεθα
ἄδικα αὐτὰ ἐργαζόμενοι, μὴ οὐ δέῃ ὑπολογίζεσθαι
οὔτ᾽ εἰ ἀποθνήσκειν δεῖ παραμένοντας καὶ ἡσυχίαν
ἄγοντας, οὔτε ἄλλο ὁτιοῦν πάσχειν πρὸ τοῦ ἀδικεῖν.

20 ΚΡ. Καλῶς μέν μοι δοκεῖς λέγειν, ὦ Σώκρατες,
ὅρα δὲ τί δρῶμεν.

ΣΩ. Σκοπῶμεν, ὦ ἀγαθέ, κοινῇ, καὶ εἴ πῃ ἔχεις
ἀντιλέγειν ἐμοῦ λέγοντος, ἀντίλεγε, καί σοι πείσομαι·
εἰ δὲ μή, παῦσαι ἤδη, ὦ μακάριε, πολλάκις μοι λέγων
25 τὸν αὐτὸν λόγον, ὡς χρὴ ἐνθένδε ἀκόντων Ἀθηναίων
ἐμὲ ἀπιέναι· ὡς ἐγὼ περὶ πολλοῦ ποιοῦμαι πεῖσαί
σε, ἀλλὰ μὴ ἄκοντος ταῦτα πράττειν. ὅρα δὲ δὴ
τῆς σκέψεως τὴν ἀρχήν, ἐάν σοι ἱκανῶς λέγηται, καὶ

49 πειρῶ ἀποκρίνεσθαι | τὸ ἐρωτώμενον, ᾗ ἂν μάλιστα
οἴῃ.   30

    ΚΡ.   Ἀλλὰ πειράσομαι.

    Χ.   ΣΩ.   Οὐδενὶ τρόπῳ φαμὲν ἑκόντας ἀδικητέον
εἶναι, ἢ τινὶ μὲν ἀδικητέον τρόπῳ, τινὶ δὲ
οὔ; ἢ οὐδαμῶς τό γε ἀδικεῖν οὔτε ἀγαθὸν
οὔτε καλόν, ὡς πολλάκις ἡμῖν καὶ ἐν τῷ
ἔμπροσθεν χρόνῳ ὡμολογήθη; ἢ πᾶσαι
ἡμῖν ἐκεῖναι αἱ πρόσθεν ὁμολογίαι ἐν
ταῖσδε ταῖς ὀλίγαις ἡμέραις ἐκκεχυμέναι
εἰσίν, καὶ πάλαι, ὦ Κρίτων, ἄρα τηλικοίδε
ἄνδρες πρὸς ἀλλήλους σπουδῇ διαλεγό-
Β μενοι ἐλάθομεν ἡμᾶς αὐτοὺς παίδων οὐδὲν   10
διαφέροντες; ἢ παντὸς μᾶλλον οὕτως ἔχει ὥσπερ
τότε ἐλέγετο ἡμῖν· εἴτε φασὶν οἱ πολλοὶ εἴτε μή, καὶ
εἴτε δεῖ ἡμᾶς ἔτι τῶνδε χαλεπώτερα πάσχειν εἴτε καὶ
πραότερα, ὅμως τό γε ἀδικεῖν τῷ ἀδικοῦντι καὶ κακὸν
καὶ αἰσχρὸν τυγχάνει ὂν παντὶ τρόπῳ; φαμὲν ἢ οὔ; 15

    ΚΡ.   Φαμέν.

    ΣΩ.   Οὐδαμῶς ἄρα δεῖ ἀδικεῖν.

    ΚΡ.   Οὐ δῆτα.

    ΣΩ.   Οὐδὲ ἀδικούμενον ἄρα ἀνταδικεῖν, ὡς οἱ
πολλοὶ οἴονται, ἐπειδή γε οὐδαμῶς δεῖ ἀδικεῖν.   20

C   ΚΡ.   Οὐ φαίνεται.

    ΣΩ.   Τί δὲ δή; κακουργεῖν δεῖ, ὦ Κρίτων, ἢ οὔ;

    ΚΡ.   Οὐ δεῖ δήπου, ὦ Σώκρατες.

    ΣΩ.   Τί δέ; ἀντικακουργεῖν κακῶς πάσχοντα,
ὡς οἱ πολλοὶ φασιν, δίκαιον ἢ οὐ δίκαιον;   25

    ΚΡ.   Οὐδαμῶς.

    ΣΩ.   Τὸ γάρ που κακῶς ποιεῖν ἀνθρώπους τοῦ
ἀδικεῖν οὐδὲν διαφέρει.

Do you still believe that we ought never to do wrong or evil to another, or requite wrong with wrong, or evil with evil? Think well before you answer: the adherents of this view cannot argue with the many, who think otherwise.' 'I still believe it.'

ΚΡ.   Ἀληθῆ λέγεις.

30 ΣΩ.   Οὔτε ἄρα ἀνταδικεῖν δεῖ οὔτε κακῶς ποιεῖν
οὐδένα ἀνθρώπων, οὐδ᾽ ἂν ὁτιοῦν πάσχῃ ὑπ᾽ αὐτῶν.
καὶ ὅρα, ὦ Κρίτων, ταῦτα καθομολογῶν, ὅπως μὴ
παρὰ δόξαν ὁμολογῇς. οἶδα γὰρ ὅτι ὀλίγοις τισὶ D
ταῦτα καὶ δοκεῖ καὶ δόξει. οἷς οὖν οὕτω δέδοκται
35 καὶ οἷς μή, τούτοις οὐκ ἔστι κοινὴ βουλή, ἀλλὰ
ἀνάγκη τούτους ἀλλήλων καταφρονεῖν, ὁρῶντας τὰ
ἀλλήλων βουλεύματα. σκόπει δὴ οὖν καὶ σὺ εὖ
μάλα πότερον κοινωνεῖς καὶ ξυνδοκεῖ σοι καὶ ἀρχώμεθα ἐντεῦθεν βουλευόμενοι, ὡς οὐδέποτε ὀρθῶς ἔχον-
40 τος οὔτε τοῦ ἀδικεῖν οὔτε τοῦ ἀνταδικεῖν οὔτε κακῶς
πάσχοντα ἀμύνεσθαι ἀντιδρῶντα κακῶς, ἢ ἀφίστασαι
καὶ οὐ κοινωνεῖς τῆς ἀρχῆς· ἐμοὶ μὲν γὰρ καὶ πάλαι E
οὕτω καὶ νῦν ἔτι δοκεῖ, σοὶ δὲ εἴ πῃ ἄλλῃ δέδοκται,
λέγε καὶ δίδασκε. εἰ δ᾽ ἐμμένεις τοῖς πρόσθε, τὸ
45 μετὰ τοῦτο ἄκουε.

ΚΡ.   Ἀλλ᾽ ἐμμένω τε καὶ ξυνδοκεῖ μοι· ἀλλὰ
λέγε.

ΣΩ.   Λέγω δὴ αὖ τὸ μετὰ τοῦτο, μᾶλλον δ᾽
ἐρωτῶ· πότερον ἃ ἄν τις ὁμολογήσῃ τῳ δίκαια ὄντα
50 ποιητέον ἢ ἐξαπατητέον;

ΚΡ.   Ποιητέον.

XI. ΣΩ.   Ἐκ τούτων δὴ ἄθρει. ἀπιόντες ἐν-
'And suppose   θένδε ἡμεῖς μὴ πείσαντες τὴν πόλιν | πό- 50
the Laws of my   τερον κακῶς τινας ποιοῦμεν, καὶ ταῦτα
country came
and accused me   οὓς ἥκιστα δεῖ, ἢ οὔ; καὶ ἐμμένομεν οἷς
of doing them
wrong, what   ὡμολογήσαμεν δικαίοις οὖσιν ἢ οὔ;
5 should I say?
Should I say
they wronged   ΚΡ.   Οὐκ ἔχω, ὦ Σώκρατες, ἀποκρί-
me first?'   νασθαι πρὸς ὃ ἐρωτᾷς· οὐ γὰρ ἐννοῶ.
'Of course.'

ΣΩ.   Ἀλλ᾽ ὧδε σκόπει. εἰ μέλλουσιν ἡμῖν ἐν-

θένδε εἴτε ἀποδιδράσκειν, εἴθ' ὅπως δεῖ ὀνομάσαι
τοῦτο, ἐλθόντες οἱ νόμοι καὶ τὸ κοινὸν τῆς πόλεως 10
ἐπιστάντες ἔροιντο· 'εἰπέ μοι, ὦ Σώκρατες, τί ἐν νῷ
ἔχεις ποιεῖν; ἄλλο τι ἢ τούτῳ τῷ ἔργῳ, ᾧ ἐπιχειρεῖς,
διανοεῖ τούς τε νόμους ἡμᾶς ἀπολέσαι καὶ ξύμπασαν
τὴν πόλιν τὸ σὸν μέρος; ἢ δοκεῖ σοι οἷόν τε ἔτι ἐκείνην τὴν πόλιν εἶναι καὶ μὴ ἀνατετράφθαι, ἐν ᾗ αἱ 15
γενόμεναι δίκαι μηδὲν ἰσχύουσιν, ἀλλὰ ὑπὸ ἰδιωτῶν
ἄκυροί τε γίγνονται καὶ διαφθείρονται;' τί ἐροῦμεν,
ὦ Κρίτων, πρὸς ταῦτα καὶ ἄλλα τοιαῦτα; πολλὰ γὰρ
ἄν τις ἔχοι, ἄλλως τε καὶ ῥήτωρ, εἰπεῖν ὑπὲρ τούτου
τοῦ νόμου ἀπολλυμένου, ὃς τὰς δίκας τὰς δικασθείσας 20
προστάττει κυρίας εἶναι. ἢ ἐροῦμεν πρὸς αὐτούς, ὅτι
ἠδίκει γὰρ ἡμᾶς ἡ πόλις καὶ οὐκ ὀρθῶς τὴν δίκην
ἔκρινεν; ταῦτα ἢ τί ἐροῦμεν;

    ΚΡ. Ταῦτα νὴ Δία, ὦ Σώκρατες.

    XII. ΣΩ. Τί οὖν, ἂν εἴπωσιν οἱ νόμοι· 'ὦ
Σώκρατες, ἢ καὶ ταῦτα ὡμολόγητο ἡμῖν
τε καὶ σοί, ἢ ἐμμένειν ταῖς δίκαις αἷς ἂν
ἡ πόλις δικάζῃ;' εἰ οὖν αὐτῶν θαυμάζοιμεν λεγόντων, ἴσως ἂν εἴποιεν ὅτι 'ὦ
Σώκρατες, μὴ θαύμαζε τὰ λεγόμενα, ἀλλ'
ἀποκρίνου, ἐπειδὴ καὶ εἴωθας χρῆσθαι
τῷ ἐρωτᾶν τε καὶ ἀποκρίνεσθαι. φέρε
γάρ, τί ἐγκαλῶν ἡμῖν καὶ τῇ πόλει ἐπιχειρεῖς ἡμᾶς
ἀπολλύναι; οὐ πρῶτον μέν σε ἐγεννήσαμεν ἡμεῖς, 10
καὶ δι' ἡμῶν ἐλάμβανεν τὴν μητέρα σου ὁ πατὴρ καὶ
ἐφύτευσέν σε; φράσον οὖν τούτοις ἡμῶν, τοῖς νόμοις
τοῖς περὶ τοὺς γάμους, μέμφει τι ὡς οὐ καλῶς ἔχουσιν;' οὐ μέμφομαι, φαίην ἄν. 'ἀλλὰ τοῖς περὶ τὴν
τοῦ γενομένου τροφήν τε καὶ παιδείαν, ἐν ᾗ καὶ σὺ 15

'They would
reply: "The bar-
gain was that you
should obey us
without any qua-
lification, as our 5
child and slave.
Persuasion you
might bring to
bear upon us, but
not force.

ἐπαιδεύθης; ἢ οὐ καλῶς προσέταττον ἡμῶν οἱ ἐπὶ
τούτοις τεταγμένοι νόμοι, παραγγέλλοντες τῷ πατρὶ
τῷ σῷ σε ἐν μουσικῇ καὶ γυμναστικῇ παιδεύειν;'
καλῶς, φαίην ἄν. 'εἶεν. ἐπειδὴ δὲ ἐγένου τε καὶ E
20 ἐξετράφης καὶ ἐπαιδεύθης, ἔχοις ἂν εἰπεῖν πρῶτον
μὲν ὡς οὐχὶ ἡμέτερος ἦσθα καὶ ἔκγονος καὶ δοῦλος,
αὐτός τε καὶ οἱ σοὶ πρόγονοι; καὶ εἰ τοῦθ' οὕτως ἔχει,
ἆρ' ἐξ ἴσου οἴει εἶναι σοὶ τὸ δίκαιον καὶ ἡμῖν, καὶ
ἅττ' ἂν ἡμεῖς σε ἐπιχειρῶμεν ποιεῖν, καὶ σοὶ ταῦτα
25 ἀντιποιεῖν οἴει δίκαιον εἶναι; ἢ πρὸς μὲν ἄρα σοι τὸν
πατέρα οὐκ ἐξ ἴσου ἦν τὸ δίκαιον καὶ πρὸς τὸν δεσπότην, εἴ σοι ὢν ἐτύγχανεν, ὥστε, ἅπερ πάσχοις, ταῦτα
καὶ ἀντιποιεῖν,—οὔτε κακῶς ἀκούοντα ἀντιλέγειν οὔτε
τυπτόμενον | ἀντιτύπτειν οὔτε ἄλλα τοιαῦτα πολλά· 5
30 πρὸς δὲ τὴν πατρίδα ἄρα καὶ τοὺς νόμους ἔσται σοι;
ὥστε, ἐὰν σὲ ἐπιχειρῶμεν ἡμεῖς ἀπολλύναι δίκαιον
ἡγούμενοι εἶναι, καὶ σὺ δὲ ἡμᾶς τοὺς νόμους καὶ τὴν
πατρίδα καθ' ὅσον δύνασαι ἐπιχειρήσεις ἀνταπολ-
λύναι, καὶ φήσεις ταῦτα ποιῶν δίκαια πράττειν, ὁ τῇ
35 ἀληθείᾳ τῆς ἀρετῆς ἐπιμελόμενος; ἢ οὕτως εἶ σοφός,
ὥστε λέληθέν σε, ὅτι μητρός τε καὶ πατρὸς καὶ τῶν
ἄλλων προγόνων ἁπάντων τιμιώτερόν ἐστιν ἡ πατρὶς
καὶ σεμνότερον καὶ ἁγιώτερον καὶ ἐν μείζονι μοίρᾳ
καὶ παρὰ θεοῖς καὶ παρ' ἀνθρώποις τοῖς νοῦν ἔχουσι,
40 καὶ σέβεσθαι δεῖ καὶ μᾶλλον ὑπείκειν καὶ θωπεύειν
πατρίδα χαλεπαίνουσαν ἢ πατέρα, καὶ ἢ πείθειν ἢ
ποιεῖν ἃ ἂν κελεύῃ, καὶ πάσχειν, ἐάν τι προστάττῃ
παθεῖν, ἡσυχίαν ἄγοντα, ἐάν τε τύπτεσθαι ἐάν τε
δεῖσθαι, ἐάν τε εἰς πόλεμον ἄγῃ τρωθησόμενον ἢ
45 ἀποθανούμενον, ποιητέον ταῦτα, καὶ τὸ δίκαιον οὕτως
ἔχει, καὶ οὐχὶ ὑπεικτέον οὐδὲ ἀναχωρητέον οὐδὲ λειπ-

τέον τὴν τάξιν, ἀλλὰ καὶ ἐν πολέμῳ καὶ ἐν δικασ-
C τηρίῳ καὶ πονταχοῦ ποιητέον, ἃ ἂν κελεύῃ ἡ πόλις
καὶ ἡ πατρίς, ἢ πείθειν αὐτὴν ᾗ τὸ δίκαιον πέφυκε,
βιάζεσθαι δὲ οὐχ ὅσιον οὔτε μητέρα οὔτε πατέρα, πολὺ 50
δὲ τούτων ἔτι ἧττον τὴν πατρίδα;' τί φήσομεν πρὸς
ταῦτα, ὦ Κρίτων; ἀληθῆ λέγειν τοὺς νόμους ἢ οὔ;

ΚΡ. Ἔμοιγε δοκεῖ.

XIII.   ΣΩ.   'Σκόπει τοίνυν, ὦ Σώκρατες,' φαῖεν
ἂν ἴσως οἱ νόμοι, 'εἰ ἡμεῖς ταῦτα ἀληθῆ
λέγομεν, ὅτι οὐ δίκαια ἡμᾶς ἐπιχειρεῖς   To remain in
δρᾶν ἃ νῦν ἐπιχειρεῖς. ἡμεῖς γάρ σε   Athens is a tacit
                                              promise to obey.
γεννήσαντες, ἐκθρέψαντες, παιδεύσαντες,   us: disobedience
                                              would be unfilial,
μεταδόντες ἀπάντων ὧν οἷοί τ᾽ ἦμεν   ungrateful and 5
                                              dishonest.
D καλῶν σοὶ καὶ τοῖς ἄλλοις πᾶσιν πολίταις, ὅμως
προαγορεύομεν τῷ ἐξουσίαν πεποιηκέναι Ἀθηναίων
τῷ βουλομένῳ, ἐπειδὰν δοκιμασθῇ καὶ ἴδῃ τὰ ἐν τῇ
πόλει πράγματα καὶ ἡμᾶς τοὺς νόμους, ᾧ ἂν μὴ 10
ἀρέσκωμεν ἡμεῖς, ἐξεῖναι λαβόντα τὰ αὑτοῦ ἀπιέναι
ὅποι ἂν βούληται. καὶ οὐδεὶς ἡμῶν τῶν νόμων ἐμ-
ποδών ἐστιν οὐδ᾽ ἀπαγορεύει, ἐάν τέ τις βούληται
ὑμῶν εἰς ἀποικίαν ἰέναι, εἰ μὴ ἀρέσκοιμεν ἡμεῖς τε
καὶ ἡ πόλις, ἐάν τε μετοικεῖν ἄλλοσε ἐλθών, ἰέναι 15
ἐκεῖσε, ὅποι ἂν βούληται, ἔχοντα τὰ αὑτοῦ. ὃς δ᾽ ἂν
E ὑμῶν παραμείνῃ, ὁρῶν ὃν τρόπον ἡμεῖς τάς τε δίκας
δικάζομεν καὶ τἆλλα τὴν πόλιν διοικοῦμεν, ἤδη φαμὲν
τοῦτον ὡμολογηκέναι ἔργῳ ἡμῖν ἃ ἂν ἡμεῖς κελεύωμεν ποιήσειν ταῦτα, καὶ τὸν μὴ πειθόμενον τριχῇ 20
φαμεν ἀδικεῖν, ὅτι τε γεννηταῖς οὖσιν ἡμῖν οὐ πείθεται, καὶ ὅτι τροφεῦσι, καὶ ὅτι ὁμολογήσας ἡμῖν πείθεσθαι οὔτε πείθεται οὔτε πείθει ἡμᾶς, εἰ μὴ καλῶς
52 τι ποιοῦμεν· προτιθέντων | ἡμῶν καὶ οὐκ ἀγρίως ἐπι-

²⁵ ταττόντων ποιεῖν ἃ ἂν κελεύωμεν, ἀλλὰ ἐφιέντων δυοῖν θάτερα, ἢ πείθειν ἡμᾶς ἢ ποιεῖν, τούτων οὐδέτερα ποιεῖ.

XIV.

In your case, Socrates, the bargain is particularly binding: no one has lived more constantly in Athens than you. Even during the trial you might have chosen exile rather than death.

Ταύταις δή φαμεν καὶ σέ, Σώκρατες, ταῖς αἰτίαις ἐνέξεσθαι, εἴπερ ποιήσεις ἃ ἐπινοεῖς, καὶ οὐχ ἥκιστα Ἀθηναίων σέ, ἀλλ' ἐν τοῖς μάλιστα.' εἰ οὖν ἐγὼ εἴποιμι· ⁵ διὰ τί δή; ἴσως ἄν μου δικαίως καθάπτοιντο λέγοντες, ὅτι ἐν τοῖς μάλιστα Ἀθηναίων ἐγὼ αὐτοῖς ὡμολογηκὼς τυγχάνω ταύτην τὴν ὁμολογίαν. φαῖεν γὰρ ἂν ὅτι 'ὦ Σώκρατες, μεγάλα ἡμῖν τούτων τεκμήριά B ¹⁰ ἐστιν, ὅτι σοι καὶ ἡμεῖς ἠρέσκομεν καὶ ἡ πόλις· οὐ γὰρ ἄν ποτε τῶν ἄλλων Ἀθηναίων ἁπάντων διαφερόντως ἐν αὐτῇ ἐπεδήμεις, εἰ μή σοι διαφερόντως ἤρεσκεν, καὶ οὔτ' ἐπὶ θεωρίαν πώποτ' ἐκ τῆς πόλεως ἐξῆλθες, οὔτε ἄλλοσε οὐδαμόσε, εἰ μή ποι στρατευ- ¹⁵ σόμενος, οὔτε ἄλλην ἀποδημίαν ἐποιήσω πώποτε, ὥσπερ οἱ ἄλλοι ἄνθρωποι, οὐδ' ἐπιθυμία σε ἄλλης πόλεως οὐδὲ ἄλλων νόμων ἔλαβεν εἰδέναι, ἀλλὰ ἡμεῖς σοι ἱκανοὶ ἦμεν καὶ ἡ ἡμετέρα πόλις· οὕτω σφόδρα C ἡμᾶς ᾑροῦ, καὶ ὡμολόγεις καθ' ἡμᾶς πολιτεύσεσθαι, ²⁰ τά τε ἄλλα καὶ παῖδας ἐν αὐτῇ ἐποιήσω, ὡς ἀρεσκούσης σοι τῆς πόλεως. ἔτι τοίνυν ἐν αὐτῇ τῇ δίκῃ ἐξῆν σοι φυγῆς τιμήσασθαι, εἰ ἐβούλου, καὶ ὅπερ νῦν ἀκούσης τῆς πόλεως ἐπιχειρεῖς, τότε ἑκούσης ποιῆσαι. σὺ δὲ τότε μὲν ἐκαλλωπίζου ὡς οὐκ ἀγανακτῶν, ²⁵ εἰ δέοι τεθνάναι σε, ἀλλὰ ᾑροῦ, ὡς ἔφησθα, πρὸ τῆς φυγῆς θάνατον· νῦν δὲ οὔτ' ἐκείνους τοὺς λόγους αἰσχύνει, οὔτε ἡμῶν τῶν νόμων ἐντρέπει, ἐπιχειρῶν διαφθεῖραι, πράττεις τε ἅπερ ἂν δοῦλος φαυλότατος D

πράξειεν, ἀποδιδράσκειν ἐπιχειρῶν παρὰ τὰς ξυνθήκας τε καὶ τὰς ὁμολογίας, καθ' ἃς ἡμῖν ξυνέθου 30
πολιτεύεσθαι.   πρῶτον μὲν οὖν ἡμῖν τοῦτ' αὐτὸ ἀπό-
κριναι, εἰ ἀληθῆ λέγομεν φάσκοντές σε ὡμολογηκέναι
πολιτεύεσθαι καθ' ἡμᾶς ἔργῳ, ἀλλ' οὐ λόγῳ, ἢ οὐκ
ἀληθῆ.'   τί φῶμεν πρὸς ταῦτα, ὦ Κρίτων; ἄλλο τι   = num
ἢ ὁμολογῶμεν;   35

KP.   Ἀνάγκη, ὦ Σώκρατες.

ΣΩ.   "Ἄλλο τι οὖν' ἂν φαῖεν 'ἢ ξυνθήκας τὰς
πρὸς ἡμᾶς αὐτοὺς καὶ ὁμολογίας παραβαίνεις, οὐχ
E ὑπὸ ἀνάγκης ὁμολογήσας οὐδὲ ἀπατηθεὶς οὐδὲ ἐν
ὀλίγῳ χρόνῳ ἀναγκασθεὶς βουλεύσασθαι, ἀλλ' ἐν 40
ἔτεσιν ἑβδομήκοντα, ἐν οἷς ἐξῆν σοι ἀπιέναι, εἰ μὴ   impossible
ἠρέσκομεν ἡμεῖς μηδὲ δίκαιαι ἐφαίνοντό σοι αἱ ὁμο-   conditions
λογίαι εἶναι; σὺ δὲ οὔτε Λακεδαίμονα προῃροῦ οὔτε
Κρήτην, ἃς δὴ ἑκάστοτε φὴς εὐνομεῖσθαι, οὔτε ἄλλην
οὐδεμίαν τῶν Ἑλληνίδων πόλεων οὐδὲ τῶν βαρβαρι- 45
3 κῶν, | ἀλλὰ ἐλάττω ἐξ αὐτῆς ἀπεδήμησας ἢ οἱ χωλοί
τε καὶ τυφλοὶ καὶ οἱ ἄλλοι ἀνάπηροι· οὕτω σοι διαφερόντως τῶν ἄλλων Ἀθηναίων ἤρεσκεν ἥ πόλις τε
καὶ ἡμεῖς οἱ νόμοι δῆλον ὅτι· τίνι γὰρ ἂν πόλις
ἀρέσκοι ἄνευ νόμων; νῦν δὲ δὴ οὐκ ἐμμένεις τοῖς 50
ὡμολογημένοις; ἐὰν ἡμῖν γε πείθῃ, ὦ Σώκρατες· καὶ
οὐ καταγέλαστός γε ἔσει ἐκ τῆς πόλεως ἐξελθών.

XV.   Σκόπει γὰρ δή, ταῦτα παραβὰς καὶ ἐξαμαρτάνων τι τούτων τί ἀγαθὸν ἐργάσει
3 σαυτὸν ἢ τοὺς ἐπιτηδείους τοὺς σαυτοῦ;
ὅτι μὲν γὰρ κινδυνεύσουσί γέ σου οἱ ἐπιτήδειοι καὶ αὐτοὶ φεύγειν καὶ στερηθῆναι
τῆς πόλεως ἢ τὴν οὐσίαν ἀπολέσαι, σχεδόν τι δῆλον· αὐτὸς δὲ πρῶτον μὲν ἐὰν

By   making
your escape, you
will   endanger
your friends. And
whither will you
flee? Wherever 5
you go, suspicion
and ridicule await
you.   Your chil-
dren too will suf-

fer more by your
escape than by
your death.
εἰς τῶν ἐγγύτατά τινα πόλεων ἔλθῃς, ἢ

Θήβαζε ἢ Μέγαράδε—εὐνομοῦνται γὰρ

10 ἀμφότεραι—πολέμιος ἥξεις, ὦ Σώκρατες, τῇ τούτων

πολιτείᾳ, καὶ ὅσοιπερ κήδονται τῶν αὑτῶν πόλεων,

ὑποβλέψονταί σε διαφθορέα ἡγούμενοι τῶν νόμων,

καὶ βεβαιώσεις τοῖς δικασταῖς τὴν δόξαν, ὥστε δοκεῖν

ὀρθῶς τὴν δίκην δικάσαι· ὅστις γὰρ νόμων διαφθο- C

15 ρεύς ἐστιν, σφόδρα που δόξειεν ἂν νέων γε καὶ ἀνοή-

των ἀνθρώπων διαφθορεὺς εἶναι. πότερον οὖν φεύξει

τάς τε εὐνομουμένας πόλεις καὶ τῶν ἀνδρῶν τοὺς

κοσμιωτάτους; καὶ τοῦτο ποιοῦντι ἆρα ἄξιόν σοι ζῆν

ἔσται; ἢ πλησιάσεις τούτοις καὶ ἀναισχυντήσεις δια-

20 λεγόμενος—τίνας λόγους, ὦ Σώκρατες; ἢ οὕσπερ

ἐνθάδε, ὡς ἡ ἀρετὴ καὶ ἡ δικαιοσύνη πλείστου ἄξιον

τοῖς ἀνθρώποις καὶ τὰ νόμιμα καὶ οἱ νόμοι; καὶ οὐκ

οἴει ἄσχημον ἂν φανεῖσθαι τὸ τοῦ Σωκράτους πρᾶγ- D

μα; οἴεσθαί γε χρή. ἀλλ' ἐκ μὲν τούτων τῶν τόπων

25 ἀπαρεῖς, ἥξεις δὲ εἰς Θετταλίαν παρὰ τοὺς ξένους

τοὺς Κρίτωνος· ἐκεῖ γὰρ δὴ πλείστη ἀταξία καὶ

ἀκολασία, καὶ ἴσως ἂν ἡδέως σου ἀκούοιεν, ὡς γελοίως

ἐκ τοῦ δεσμωτηρίου ἀπεδίδρασκες σκευήν τέ τινα

περιθέμενος ἢ διφθέραν λαβὼν ἢ ἄλλα οἷα δὴ εἰώθα-

30 σιν ἐνσκευάζεσθαι οἱ ἀποδιδράσκοντες, καὶ τὸ σχῆμα

τὸ σαυτοῦ μεταλλάξας· ὅτι δὲ γέρων ἀνὴρ σμικροῦ

χρόνου τῷ βίῳ λοιποῦ ὄντος, ὡς τὸ εἰκός, ἐτόλμησας E

οὕτως αἰσχρῶς ἐπιθυμεῖν ζῆν, νόμους τοὺς μεγίστους

παραβάς, οὐδεὶς ὃς ἐρεῖ; ἴσως, ἂν μή τινα λυπῇς· εἰ

35 δὲ μή, ἀκούσει, ὦ Σώκρατες, πολλὰ καὶ ἀνάξια σαυ-

τοῦ. ὑπερχόμενος δὴ βιώσει πάντας ἀνθρώπους καὶ

δουλεύων· τί ποιῶν ἢ εὐωχούμενος ἐν Θετταλίᾳ,

ὥσπερ ἐπὶ δεῖπνον ἀποδεδημηκὼς εἰς Θετταλίαν;

λόγοι δὲ ἐκεῖνοι οἱ περὶ δικαιοσύνης τε καὶ τῆς ἄλλης
54 ἀρετῆς ποῦ ἡμῖν | ἔσονται; ἀλλὰ δὴ τῶν παίδων 40
ἕνεκα βούλει ζῆν, ἵνα αὐτοὺς ἐκθρέψῃς καὶ παιδεύσῃς.
τί δέ; εἰς Θετταλίαν αὐτοὺς ἀγαγὼν θρέψεις τε καὶ
παιδεύσεις, ξένους ποιήσας, ἵνα καὶ τοῦτο ἀπολαύσωσιν; ἢ τοῦτο μὲν οὔ, αὐτοῦ δὲ τρεφόμενοι σοῦ ζῶντος
βέλτιον θρέψονται καὶ παιδεύσονται, μὴ ξυνόντος σοῦ 45
αὐτοῖς; οἱ γὰρ ἐπιτήδειοι οἱ σοὶ ἐπιμελήσονται αὐτῶν.
πότερον ἐὰν εἰς Θετταλίαν ἀποδημήσῃς, ἐπιμελήσονται, ἐὰν δὲ εἰς Ἅιδου ἀποδημήσῃς, οὐχὶ ἐπιμελή-
B σονται; εἴπερ γέ τι ὄφελος αὐτῶν ἐστιν τῶν σοι
φασκόντων ἐπιτηδείων εἶναι, οἴεσθαί γε χρή.   50

XVI. Ἀλλ᾽, ὦ Σώκρατες, πειθόμενος ἡμῖν τοῖς
σοῖς τροφεῦσι μήτε παῖδας περὶ πλείονος
ποιοῦ μήτε τὸ ζῆν μήτε ἄλλο μηδὲν πρὸ   It is well for
you to die now, in
τοῦ δικαίου, ἵνα εἰς Ἅιδου ἐλθὼν ἔχῃς   view both of this
present world and
πάντα ταῦτα ἀπολογήσασθαι τοῖς ἐκεῖ   of the next. Do
                                         not let Crito per- 5
ἄρχουσιν· οὔτε γὰρ ἐνθάδε σοι φαίνεται   suade you."
ταῦτα πράττοντι ἄμεινον εἶναι οὐδὲ δικαιότερον οὐδὲ
ὁσιώτερον, οὐδὲ ἄλλῳ τῶν σῶν οὐδενί, οὔτε ἐκεῖσε
ἀφικομένῳ ἄμεινον ἔσται. ἀλλὰ νῦν μὲν ἠδικημένος
C ἄπει, ἐὰν ἀπίῃς, οὐχ ὑφ᾽ ἡμῶν τῶν νόμων ἀλλὰ ὑπὸ 10
ἀνθρώπων· ἐὰν δὲ ἐξέλθῃς οὕτως αἰσχρῶς ἀνταδικήσας τε καὶ ἀντικακουργήσας, τὰς σαυτοῦ ὁμολογίας τε καὶ ξυνθήκας τὰς πρὸς ἡμᾶς παραβὰς καὶ
κακὰ ἐργασάμενος τούτους οὓς ἥκιστα ἔδει, σαυτόν τε
καὶ φίλους καὶ πατρίδα καὶ ἡμᾶς, ἡμεῖς τέ σοι χαλε- 15
πανοῦμεν ζῶντι, καὶ ἐκεῖ οἱ ἡμέτεροι ἀδελφοὶ οἱ ἐν
Ἅιδου νόμοι οὐκ εὐμενῶς σε ὑποδέξονται, εἰδότες ὅτι
καὶ ἡμᾶς ἐπεχείρησας ἀπολέσαι τὸ σὸν μέρος. ἀλλὰ
D μή σε πείσῃ Κρίτων ποιεῖν ἃ λέγει μᾶλλον ἢ ἡμεῖς.᾽

XVII.

This, Crito, is
what I seem to
hear them saying.
Have you any-
thing more to
urge?' 'No-
thing.' 'Then
let us act as God
directs.'

Ταῦτα, ὦ φίλε ἑταῖρε Κρίτων, εὖ ἴσθι
ὅτι ἐγὼ δοκῶ ἀκούειν, ὥσπερ οἱ κορυβαντιῶντες τῶν αὐλῶν δοκοῦσιν ἀκούειν, καὶ
ἐν ἐμοὶ αὕτη ἡ ἠχὴ τούτων τῶν λόγων
βομβεῖ καὶ ποιεῖ μὴ δύνασθαι τῶν ἄλλων
ἀκούειν· ἀλλὰ ἴσθι, ὅσα γε τὰ νῦν ἐμοὶ
δοκοῦντα, ἐὰν λέγῃς παρὰ ταῦτα, μάτην ἐρεῖς. ὅμως
μέντοι εἴ τι οἴει πλέον ποιήσειν λέγε.

ΚΡ. Ἀλλ', ὦ Σώκρατες, οὐκ ἔχω λέγειν.

ΣΩ. Ἔα τοίνυν, ὦ Κρίτων, καὶ πράττωμεν ταύτῃ, E
ἐπειδὴ ταύτῃ ὁ θεὸς ὑφηγεῖται.

NOTES.

Κρίτων [ἢ περὶ πρακτέου. ἠθικός] In the MSS of Plato each
dialogue generally has two or even three titles: the Bodleian MS for
example denotes the other three members of the first Tetralogy by
the names Εὐθύφρων ἢ περὶ ὁσίου. πειραστικός, Ἀπολογία Σωκράτους.
ἠθικός, Φαίδων ἢ περὶ ψυχῆς. ἠθικός. In each case only the first of
these titles dates from Plato, who generally (but not always) named
the dialogue after one of the characters appearing in it. The second
title was added by Thrasylus, a rhetorician and literary critic who
flourished about the Christian era: it is intended to explain the subject treated of in the dialogue. It is not clear whether the third
title was added, as Grote believes (Plato Vol. I. p. 160), by
Thrasylus, or by Diogenes Laertius either on his own responsibility
or in obedience to some other authority (see Diog. Laert. III. 49);
at all events it is meant to indicate the formal scope of the dialogue
—whether a dialogue of exposition (ὑφηγητικός, of which ἠθικός is a
subdivision), or a dialogue of search (ζητητικός). Here the Crito
is correctly described as an ethical dialogue dealing with a question
of duty (περὶ πρακτέου: cf. 46 B σκοπεῖσθαι οὖν χρὴ ἡμᾶς εἴτε ταῦτα
πρακτέον εἴτε μή)—viz. is it right to save one's life by breaking
the law?

Crito was one of Socrates' oldest and most attached friends (Apol.
33 D, Phaedo 115 A foll.). He appears to have been rich and not
indisposed to make more money (Euthyd. 304 C). The fact that he
had stood surety for Socrates after the trial (Phaedo 115 D) increased
his personal danger if Socrates should escape from prison, and
reveals in a yet stronger light his devotion to his friend: see note
on 45 D. "Plato's picture of Crito is as of a sensible and kindly
man of the world, looking upon life from the point of view of an
honest Athenian gentleman, but without any capacity for philosophy".—Archer-Hind's Phaedo p. 42.

The scene is in the prison, just before daybreak.

CHAPTER I.

Crito warns Socrates that the ship is on its way back from Delos, and will arrive to-day.

43 A   1. **τηνικάδε** = 'at this hour')(*τηνίκα* 'at that hour': so *τοιόσδε* = 'of this sort')(*τοῖος* 'of that sort'. The distinction is like that between ὅδε and οὗτος. *τηνίκα* seems to have been originally a Doric adverb (*τῆνος* is Doric for ἐκεῖνος): the suffix reappears in αὐτ-ίκα.

2. **πρῴ**. Socrates is not surprised to see Crito, for we learn from the Phaedo (59 D, cf. Xen. Mem. IV. 8. 2) that he was daily visited by his friends during the interval between his condemnation and his death: but he is surprised to see him *so early*. The prison was generally opened somewhat later (ἀνεῴγετο γὰρ οὐ πρῴ Phaed. l. c.). **πρῴ** and not **πρωΐ** is the correct Attic form of this word. The Bodleian has *πρωΐ*.

3. **πάνυ μὲν οὖν** = 'imo, valde quidem' (Göbel). *μὲν οὖν* is corrective: see on Apol. 26 B and cf. infra 44 B ἄτοπον τὸ ἐνύπνιον, ὦ Σώκρατες. Ἐναργὲς μὲν οὖν.

4. **πηνίκα μάλιστα.** *πηνίκα* means 'at what precise time?' *πότε* only 'at what time?' *μάλιστα* makes the question more vague: 'About what o'clock is it?' So τί μάλιστα; = quid potissimum? Gorg. 448 D.

5. **ὄρθρος βαθύς** = 'just before daybreak': so Prot. 310 A ἔτι βαθέος ὄρθρου, Ar. Vesp. 216 ἀλλὰ νῦν ὄρθρος βαθύς. *ὄρθρος* is the morning twilight, and *βαθύς* implies that it was more dark than light: cf. the expressions βαθεῖα νύξ, βαθεῖα ἑσπέρα.

6. **θαυμάζω ὅπως.** Stallbaum quotes Xen. Mem. I. 1. 20 θαυμάζω οὖν ὅπως ποτὲ ἐπείσθησαν Ἀθηναῖοι κτλ. The idiom means 'I wonder how it was that etc.': θαυμάζω εἰ would mean 'I wonder that'. Infra **σοι—ὑπακοῦσαι** = 'to let you in': ὑπακούειν is often used of answering the door: cf. Phaed. 59 E ὁ θυρωρὸς ὅσπερ εἰώθει ὑπακούειν and ὁ ὑπακούσας of the porter in Xen. Symp. I. 11.

8. **διὰ τὸ πολλάκις δεῦρο φοιτᾶν.** Socrates' friends generally met in the δικαστήριον, which adjoined the prison (Phaed. 59 D), and waited till the prison was opened.

9. **εὐηργέτηται.** Where initial εὐ- or οἰ- precede a vowel in Attic verbs, "that vowel, and not the initial diphthong, receives the augment. Thus—εὐηγγελιζόμην, εὐηργέτουν, εὐωδώθην, εὐώρκουν" (Rutherford, New Phrynichus, p. 245). "τι is equivalent to εὐερ-

γεσίαν τινὰ (a tip)" Dyer. καί—καί above is 'and also.' [B and the editors[1], except Kral, read εὐεργέτηται.]

12. ἐπιεικῶς πάλαι = 'some little time'. Theaet. 142 A ἄρτι— ἢ πάλαι ἐξ ἀγροῦ; 'Επιεικῶς πάλαι.

13. εἶτα. On εἶτα indignabundum see Apol. 28 B (εἶτ' οὐκ 43 B αἰσχύνει;) and my note there. For εἶτα followed by πῶς cf. (with Stallbaum) Eur. Iph. Aul. 894 κᾆτα πῶς φέρων γε δέλτον οὐκ ἐμοὶ δίδως λαβεῖν;

15. οὐ μὰ τὸν Δία κτλ. = 'no! Socrates, believe me, I could wish that I myself were not so sleepless and sorrowful'. οὐ does not anticipate the following οὐδέ in οὐδ' ἂν αὐτός (ne ipse quidem), but is part of Crito's reply to Socrates' question, since εἶτα—παρακάθησαι = ἐχρῆν εὐθὺς ἐπεγείραί με, ἀλλὰ μὴ σιγῇ παρακαθῆσθαι. For the displacement of τε Stallbaum compares Phaed. 94 D τά τε κατὰ τὴν γυμναστικὴν καὶ τὴν ἰατρικήν. Wohlrab takes οὐ as merely anticipatory of the following negative: I agree with Göbel.

17. ἀλλὰ καὶ σοῦ—θαυμάζω sc. just as *you* were lately surprised, supra 43 A θαυμάζω ὅπως κτλ. For θαυμάζω with gen. see Goodwin's Greek Grammar p. 222. Cron on the other hand takes ἀλλὰ καί as = 'but furthermore', while Göbel connects καὶ θαυμάζω with καὶ οὐκ ἤγειρον in the next line—'both—and'.

18. οὐκ ἤγειρον. The rest of Crito's reply to Socrates' πῶς οὐκ εὐθὺς ἐπήγειράς με κτλ. By using the conjunctive διάγῃς where at first sight we should expect the optative διάγοις in the next line, Crito contrives to indicate that he still wishes Socrates ὡς ἥδιστα διάγειν: cf. Rep. V. 472 C παραδείγματος ἄρα ἕνεκα—ἐζητοῦμεν αὐτό τε δικαιοσύνην οἷόν ἐστι—ἵνα—ἀναγκαζώμεθα καὶ περὶ ἡμῶν αὐτῶν ὁμολογεῖν. In Apol. 40 D Socrates declares that nothing is ἄμεινον καὶ ἥδιον than sound dreamless sleep.

19. καὶ—μὲν δή—καί = 'yes, and': so also καὶ μὲν δὴ καί—γε in Rep. V. 464 B.

20. ηὐδαιμόνισα τοῦ τρόπου. Inscriptions of the age of Plato shew that verbs beginning with εὐ- regularly had an augment in the secondary tenses: see Rutherford New Phryn. 244 and Meisterhans, Grammatik der Attischen Inschriften 78. Here the MSS and edd. (except Kral) read εὐδαιμόνισα. On the genitive with εὐδαιμονίζειν compare Goodwin's Greek Grammar p. 224: and for the sentiment

---

[1] By "the editors" I mean Cron, Schanz, Wohlrab, Göbel and Kral: see Preface.

Phaed. 58 E εὐδαίμων γάρ μοι ἀνὴρ ἐφαίνετο—καὶ τοῦ τρόπου καὶ τῶν λόγων.

21. **ὡς ῥᾳδίως** i.q. ὅτι οὕτω ῥᾳδίως (Cron).

24. **τηλικοῦτον ὄντα.** Socrates was seventy years of age: v. infra 52 E.

43 C   26. **ἁλίσκονται ἐν** = 'are overtaken by' (Church). In this sense ἁλίσκεσθαι more often takes the dative without ἐν.

οὐδὲν—ἐπιλύεται—τὸ μὴ οὐχὶ ἀγανακτεῖν = 'in no way saves them from being indignant'. Verbs of hindering, if negative themselves, are regularly followed by μὴ οὐ with the infinitive, which may or may not have the article. Goodwin MT. 198 foll. With the present example compare Rep. I. 354 B οὐκ ἀπεσχόμην τὸ μὴ οὐκ—ἐλθεῖν and Aesch. Prom. 918 οὐδὲν γὰρ αὐτῷ ταῦτ' ἐπαρκέσει τὸ μὴ οὐ πεσεῖν ἀτίμως κτλ. Whitelaw (Transactions of the Cambridge Philological Society III. I, p. 41 foll.) endeavours, I think with success, to prove that both negatives have a value, the infinitive being consecutive. Thus while ἐκώλυσεν ἐμὲ μὴ εἰπεῖν = 'he hindered me, so that I did not speak', οὐκ ἐκώλυσεν ἐμὲ μὴ οὐκ εἰπεῖν = 'he did not hinder me, so that I did not refrain-from-speaking' i.e. keep silence (οὐκ εἰπεῖν).

29. **ἀλλὰ τί δή.** ἀλλά reverts to 43 A τί τηνικάδε ἀφῖξαι, ὦ Κρίτων; on πρῴ v. note ibid.

34. **ἐν τοῖς βαρύτατα.** Note the climax: χαλεπήν—χαλεπὴν καὶ βαρεῖαν—ἐν τοῖς βαρύτατα. The phrase ἐν τοῖς adds emphasis to the superlative. When occurring with the superlative of adjectives, it is best explained by supplying a fresh superlative to agree with the article: this superlative is sometimes expressed, e.g. Cratyl. 427 E ὃ δὴ δοκεῖ ἐν τοῖς μεγίστοις μέγιστον εἶναι (so the best MSS, but Schanz rejects μεγίστοις): compare also the kindred expression in Symp. 195 E ἐν μαλακωτάτοις τῶν μαλακωτάτων. When as here the phrase is linked to an adverb, we must repeat the superlative along with a participle supplied from the verb to which the adverb belongs: thus ἐν τοῖς βαρύτατα ἂν ἐνέγκαιμι = ἐν τοῖς βαρύτατα φέρουσιν βαρύτατ' ἂν ἐνέγκαιμι. In Thucydides the phrase has become purely adverbial and may be used even with feminine adjectives, as in the well-known ἐν τοῖς πλεῖσται δὴ νῆες III. 17, where see Classen's note. Compare Kühner, Griechische Grammatik II. 27.

35. **τίνα ταύτην;** sc. φέρων ἀφῖξαι. ἤ is the Latin an? See my note on Apol. 26 B. The annual mission to Delos, during

which no criminal was put to death at Athens, had begun the day
before Socrates' trial, when the priest of Apollo decorated the bow
of the vessel with garlands. On this occasion the boat was absent
thirty days. The mission was intended to commemorate the de-
liverance of Athens under Theseus from the annual tribute of young
men and maidens sent to Crete: see Phaed 58 A foll. and Xen.
Mem. IV. 8. 2.

36. τεθνάναι is slightly more emphatic than ἀποθνήσκειν: see
on Apol. 30 C οὐδ' εἰ μέλλω πολλάκις τεθνάναι, and infr. 52 C.
The infinitive θνήσκειν is hardly used by good Attic prose writers,
ἀποθνήσκειν being used instead: but τέθνηκα, ἐτεθνήκη are alone
right, never ἀποτέθνηκα, ἀπετεθνήκη   Rutherford Babrius p. 36.

37. οὔ τοι δὴ ἀφῖκται = 'no, it is true that it has not arrived'.   43 D

δοκεῖ μέν μοι ἥξειν. So I read with the second hand in B and
most of the editors: Schanz reads δοκεῖν μέν μοι ἥξει. With δοκεῖν,
as with the Latin videri, the personal construction is generally
preferred: if we follow Schanz δοκεῖν μέν μοι is to be taken as an
infinitive used absolutely = 'in my opinion': cf. Ar. Aves 1235
δεινότατα γάρ τοι πεισόμεσθ', ἐμοὶ δοκεῖν, and κατὰ τοῦτο εἶναι in
Prot. 317 A (ἐγὼ δὲ τούτοις ἅπασι κατὰ τοῦτο εἶναι οὐ ξυμφέρομαι),
and the common phrase ἑκὼν εἶναι. The construction δοκεῖ μέν μοι
ἥξει though rare is also allowable: see Phaed. 108 D ὁ βίος μοι
δοκεῖ ὁ ἐμός — τῷ μήκει τοῦ λόγου οὐκ ἐξαρκεῖ, and compare (with
Schanz, Novae Commentationes p. 130) Menex. 236 B ὅτε μοι δοκεῖ
συνετίθει τὸν ἐπιτάφιον λόγον: see also infra on 50 B. For μέν (after
δοκεῖ) without a following δέ—a frequent idiom in a clause with
ἀλλά, the antithesis to which is really contained in the preceding
negative clause—compare (with Stallbaum) Prot. 344 A οὐ γὰρ εἶναι,
ἀλλὰ γενέσθαι μέν ἐστιν κτλ.

39. Σουνίου. Homer Od. III. 278 Σούνιον ἱρὸν — ἄκρον Ἀθηνέων
(Fischer). Cape Sunium was the great landmark for seamen on the
South coast of Attica.

40. ἀγγέλων viz. the ἥκοντές τινες. ἄγγελοι in the sense of
'news' (nuntii) is not found before Polybius. ἐκ before ἀγγέλων is
like ἐκ of the agent (conceived of as the source) after passive verbs,
e.g. Tim. 47 B δωρηθὲν ἐκ θεῶν. Wohlrab and Kral read ἀγγελιῶν
with some MSS: Cron, Schanz and Göbel bracket τῶν ἀγγέλων, on
the ground that ἀγγέλων cannot = ἀγγελιῶν, and that ἐκ to express
the source must be followed by a neuter or inanimate object: but
the example I have cited is enough to defend the idiom.

A. C.   4

CHAPTER II.

Socrates relying on a vision declares that the ship will not arrive till to-morrow.

1. **τύχῃ ἀγαθῇ** sc. εἴη=quod bene vortat: 'I pray that it may be for the best'. The formula is frequent on inscriptions and decrees: see Thucydides IV. 118 ἔδοξεν τῷ δήμῳ.—Λάχης εἶπε, τύχῃ ἀγαθῇ τῇ Ἀθηναίων ποιεῖσθαι τὴν ἐκεχειρίαν. Pl. Symp. 177 E ἀλλὰ τύχῃ ἀγαθῇ καταρχέτω Φαῖδρος. With εἰ ταύτῃ τοῖς θεοῖς φίλον, ταύτῃ ἔστω compare the last words of the dialogue: πράττωμεν ταύτῃ, ἐπειδὴ ταύτῃ ὁ θεὸς ὑφηγεῖται.

44 A   5. **τῇ γάρ που.** This is the introductory γάρ (γ᾽ ἄρα) and should not be translated: see on Apol. 20 E Χαιρεφῶντα γὰρ ἴστε που.

6. **ὑστεραίᾳ—ἢ ῇ.** "ἡ προτεραία et ἡ ὑστεραία perpetuo usu de *diebus* dicuntur, omisso semper ἡμέρα—προτέρα et ὑστέρα de aliis rebus quibuslibet repetitis, concione, proelio etc." Cobet, Variae Lectiones 246. The words are often confused with one another in MSS. ὑστεραία being a virtual comparative is followed by ῇ. Note the orthography in ἀποθνήσκειν: the ι is found in B here and infra 46 D and 48 D: inscriptions also furnish evidence to the same effect: see Meisterhans, Grammatik der Attischen Inschriften p. 86. θνήσκω is connected with θείνω, φόνος, Skt. *han:* the ending -ίσκω is probably on the analogy of στερ-ίσκω, ἀλίσκομαι and the like. Compare Gust. Meyer, Griech. Gr.² pp. 259, 451.

7. **γέ τοι δή.** γέ τοι = 'at all events'.

οἱ τούτων κύριοι viz. οἱ ἕνδεκα, the board of eleven (ten ordinary members and a γραμματεύς) who had general charge of the prisons and saw that the capital sentence was carried out: Phaed. 59 E, 116 B foll.

9. **τῆς ἑτέρας** 'to-morrow' i.e. the second day)(τῆς ἐπιούσης or that which was just beginning. Soph. O. T. 781 τὴν μὲν οὖσαν ἡμέραν μόλις κατέσχον θατέρᾳ δ᾽ ἰὼν πέλας μητρὸς πατρός τ᾽ ἤλεγχον. From Phaedo 59 D—E it appears that Socrates was right: the boat did not arrive till the second day.

10. **ταύτης τῆς νυκτός:** genitive of time within which: Goodwin, Gk. Gr. 227.

11. κινδυνεύεις in the sense of δοκεῖς: so frequently in conversational style.

ἐν καιρῷ τινι 'peropportune' (Stallbaum). τις, as Cron remarks, has the effect of a litotes: cf. εἶχον ἄν τινα λόγον Apol. 31 B.

οὐκ ἐγεῖραι. Not μὴ ἐγεῖραι, because οὐκ ἐγεῖραι is a single notion: compare 43 B καὶ ἐπίτηδές σε οὐκ ἤγειρον.

13. ἦν δὲ δὴ τί τὸ ἐνύπνιον = 'but about the vision—what was it?' For the order compare λέγω δὲ δὴ τί τοῦτο; Symp. 178 D. Socrates was greatly influenced by dreams and oracles and μαντική generally: see Apol. 33 C ἐμοὶ δὲ τοῦτο ὡς ἐγὼ φημι προστέτακται ὑπὸ τοῦ θεοῦ πράττειν καὶ ἐκ μαντείων καὶ ἐξ ἐνυπνίων κτλ. The story of this vision is also told (inaccurately) by Diogenes Laertius, II. 5. 35, and referred to in Cic. de Div. I. 52. For two other examples see Phaed. 60 E and Diog. Laert. III. 5. In his respect for divination Socrates presents the most striking contrast to Plato, who places priestcraft and divination in the lowest of the three classes of arts distinguished in the Politicus (290 C foll.). See on this subject Nohle's excellent essay "Die Statslehre Platos in ihrer geschichtlichen Entwicklung", Jena, 1880.

14. γυνὴ—καλὴ καὶ εὐειδής. Wohlrab points out that a robe of white was significant of joy: compare Legg. XII. 947 B, where Plato in speaking of funerals ordains λευκὴν μὲν τὴν στολὴν ἔχειν πᾶσαν, θρήνων δὲ καὶ ὀδυρμῶν χωρὶς γίγνεσθαι. So in Aeschylus Pers. 301 λευκὸν ἦμαρ νυκτὸς ἐκ μελαγχίμου. Probably Socrates identified the vision with ἡ εἰμαρμένη: see Phaed. 115 A ἐμὲ δὲ νῦν ἤδη καλεῖ, φαίη ἂν ἀνὴρ τ᾽, ἀγικός, ἡ εἱμαρμένη.

16. ἤματί κεν τριτάτῳ κτλ. after Il. IX. 363 ἤματί κε τριτάτῳ 44 B Φθίην ἐρίβωλον ἱκοίμην, spoken by Achilles. It is possible (as Cron suggests) that the meaning of the line for Socrates lay partly in the fact that Phthia was the *home* of Achilles: but I feel sure that (rightly or wrongly) Socrates associated Φθίη with φθίω and φθίσις, and derived comfort from the epithet ἐρίβωλον. In Euripides' Electra 836 there is what seems to me a similar play upon the word Φθίας. Orestes has been dissecting a victim with a Δωρικὴ κοπίς, in the presence of Aegisthus. Suddenly he lays it aside and exclaims: οὐχ, ὅπως παστήρια θοιvασόμεσθα, Φθιάδ᾽ ἀντὶ Δωρικῆς οἴσει τις ἡμῖν κοπίδα; With this Φθιὰς κοπίς he slays Aegisthus. I am glad to find that Lambinus (as a pupil has pointed out to me) took the same view of Φθίην in this passage. See also infra on 47 B line 14.

18. **ἄτοπον τὸ ἐνύπνιον.** ὡς ἄτοπον τὸ ἐνύπνιον is an inferior reading.

19. **ἐναργὲς μὲν οὖν** 'No, it is *plain*': on μὲν οὖν (immo) v. above 43 A πάνυ μὲν οὖν.

CHAPTER III.

Crito entreats Socrates to escape and save the reputation of his friend.

1. **ὦ δαιμόνιε Σώκρατες.** ὦ δαιμόνιε was a favourite mode of address in Athenian society. The adjective meant originally 'more than human': in Homer it is generally used as an epithet of reproach, in Attic, of affection coupled with remonstrance (as here), or ironically. ὦ μακάριε is used in the same way. Other kindred expressions are ὦ βέλτιστε, ὦ ἄριστε, ὦ λῷστε, ὦ θαυμάσιε: the three first mean 'my excellent friend' or 'my fine fellow' (ironical): the last 'my dear sir' (with remonstrance). Often the precise shade of meaning can only be conveyed by the tone of the voice in translating aloud.

2. **ἔτι καὶ νῦν.** The words imply that Crito had already made many attempts to induce Socrates to escape: cf. infra 48 E παῦσαι ἤδη—πολλάκις μοι λέγων τὸν αὐτὸν λόγον, ὡς χρὴ ἐνθένδε ἀκόντων Ἀθηναίων ἐμὲ ἀπιέναι. ἔτι καὶ νῦν means 'even at the eleventh hour': cf. Ar. Ran 1235 ἀλλ᾽ ὦγάθ᾽ ἔτι καὶ νῦν ἀπόδος. For the collocation of present and aorist in πείθου καὶ σώθητι cf. Gorg. 486 c where the mss read ἐμοὶ πείθου, παῦσαι δ᾽ ἐλέγχων.

3. **οὐ μία** =non una='more than one'. The Bodleian has οὐδεμία: but this can hardly be right. Crito proceeds to enumerate two misfortunes: the loss of his friend and the loss of his reputation. Observe that Crito thinks his reputation will suffer more if Socrates remains to die than if he breaks his own pledge to the Athenian people by inducing Socrates to escape: see Phaed. 115 D. In Crito's judgment (and Crito here as elsewhere represents the average Athenian gentleman of the day) it is a higher duty to serve one's friend than to be true to one's country. It is this point of view which Socrates combats in the sequel, as utterly fatal to the very existence of the State.

4. **χωρὶς μὲν—ἀμελῆσαι.** I have retained the reading of the Bodleian, which all the recent editors have changed. χωρίς is an adverb, as the balance between χωρὶς μέν and ἔτι δέ proves (see also Madvig Adv. I. 369): to regard it as a preposition makes it necessary either to insert τοῦ before σοῦ (as Ast does), or to change σοῦ to τοῦ with most editors. If we follow the MSS, the construction is ἀλλὰ χωρὶς μὲν (on the one hand) <ἐμοί ἐστιν> σοῦ ἐστερῆσθαι, τοιούτου ἐπιτηδείου—ἔτι δέ κτλ. ἔτι δέ is substituted for χωρὶς δέ in the second half of the antithesis because χωρὶς δέ would require καὶ πολλοῖς δοκεῖν <sc. ἐμοί ἐστιν> to balance χωρὶς μὲν σοῦ ἐστερῆσθαι: this would be awkward, with ἐστίν so far removed. For χωρὶς μέν followed by χωρὶς δέ compare Parm. 130 B. There is however much to be said for reading τοῦ, not σοῦ†. Translate the whole sentence as it stands thus: 'For to me your death is more than a single calamity: on the one hand, there is the loss of you, a friend such as I shall never find again, and moreover many men, who do not know you and me well, will think me guilty of neglect, because I might have saved you, if I had been willing to spend money'. ὡς οἷός τ' ὢν is explanatory of ἀμελῆσαι.

5. **ἐστερῆσθαι.** στέρομαι and its kindred forms have two senses in Plato as in Attic generally: either 'I am debarred from', or 'I am deprived of': an example of the former meaning is Rep. VI. 484 C οἱ τῷ ὄντι τοῦ ὄντος ἑκάστου ἐστερημένοι τῆς γνώσεως: for the latter cf. Phaed. 117 D οἵου ἀνδρὸς ἑταίρου ἐστερημένος εἴην.

6. **οὐδένα μήποτε εὑρήσω** i.q. οὐ μήποτέ τινα εὑρήσω. εὑρήσω is of course future. οὐ μή with the future indicative (rare), or (far more often) the aorist conjunctive (cf. infr. 46 C οὐ μή σοι ξυγχωρήσω), is a strong negative: for the sense of futurity in the aorist conjunctive compare πί-ο-μαι, ἔδ-ο-μαι (conjunctives with the short vowel as in ἀλλ' ἴ-ο-μεν) and perhaps Latin faxo, i.e. fac-s-o: see my note on Apol. 29 D and compare Goodwin MT. p. 184.

7. **οἳ—μὴ ἴσασιν.** Not οἳ—ου because the clause is virtually conditional: no one who knew Crito and Socrates well could imagine that Crito had treated him with neglect.

ὡς οἷός τ' ὢν σε σῴζειν = 'because' (in *their* opinion, whence ὡς) 'I might have saved you'. This clause is explained by ἀμελῆσαι: it was *because* Crito had the money, and didn't use it, that ignorant men might charge him with neglect: had he been penniless, he would have escaped the charge. Crito was very well off: see Eu-

---

† This view is taken by Otto Apelt in a review of my first Edition in the 'Berliner Philologische Wochenschrift' for Dec. 15, 1888.

thyd. 304 C. Cron and Göbel take ὡς to mean 'although': so Schanz
in Zeitschrift für die österreichischen Gymnasien, Vol. 20 (1869)
p. 87, comparing the concessive use of ἐπεί or ἐπεί—γε in Prot.
317 A οὐ γὰρ λαθεῖν τῶν ἀνθρώπων τοὺς δυναμένους—ὧνπερ ἕνεκα ταῦτ'
ἐστὶ τὰ προσχήματα, ἐπεί οἵ γε πολλοί—οὐδὲν αἰσθάνονται : but it is
only in the modern idiom that even this use of ἐπεί is concessive: to
the Greeks it was causal, 'for, as for the many, they etc.' Note the
iota subscript in σῴζειν : it is regularly found in the present stem of
this verb down to 160 B.C.: see Meisterhans, Grammatik der
Attischen Inschriften, p. 87.

44 C   9. ταύτης—ἢ δοκεῖν = 'than this, than to be thought'. ταύτης
refers forward, not to δοκεῖν, but to ἢ δοκεῖν. For a similar case see
Gorg. 500 C οὐ τί ἂν μᾶλλον σπουδάσειέ τις καὶ σμικρὸν νοῦν ἔχων ἄν-
θρωπος, ἢ τοῦτο κτλ. and Cicero De Fin. I. 19 quo nihil turpius
physico, quam fieri quicquam sine causa dicere. For the repetition
of δοκεῖν after δόξα compare infr. 53 B βεβαιώσεις τοῖς δικασταῖς τὴν
δόξαν, ὥστε δοκεῖν ὀρθῶς τὴν δίκην δικάσαι.

10. χρήματα περὶ πλείονος ποιεῖσθαι ἢ φίλους. Socrates had
himself very lofty views on the subject of friendship: see Mem. II.
4. 5 καί τοι πρὸς ποῖον κτῆμα τῶν ἄλλων παραβαλλόμενος φίλος ἀγαθὸς
οὐκ ἂν πολλῷ κρείττων φανείη; ibid. § 1 he censures the many for
saying that a true and good friend is the best of all possessions, and
yet caring more for money than for friends.

13. ὦ μακάριε Κρίτων. See on ὦ δαιμόνιε supra 44 B.

τῆς τῶν πολλῶν δόξης. Socrates everywhere insisted that the
opinion of the many is worthless, in comparison with that of the
man who knows: see my introduction to the Apology p. x. and the
passages there cited.

15. φροντίζειν with a genitive, as often in Plato, e.g. Soph.
246 D ἡμεῖς δὲ οὐ τούτων φροντίζομεν, ἀλλὰ τἀληθὲς ζητοῦμεν.

αὐτά is frequently used, without any expressed antecedent, for the
matter under discussion, e.g. 46 C πῶς οὖν ἂν μετριώτατα σκοποίμεθα
αὐτά; Gorg. 509 E ἢ καὶ ἐπὶ τοῦτο δεῖ δύναμιν καὶ τέχνην παρασκευά-
σασθαι, ὡς, ἐὰν μὴ μάθῃ αὐτὰ καὶ ἀσκήσῃ, ἀδικήσει;

44 D   18. αὐτὰ δὲ δῆλα. This use of αὐτά throws light on αὐτίκα
(from αὐτός) in the sense of 'for example'. δῆλα (sc. ἐστίν) is passive:
so in Rep. I. 348 E νῦν δὲ δῆλος εἶ ὅτι φήσεις: the idiom is like 'I
see thee, who thou art'. As to the omission of the copula it should
be noted that Plato rarely leaves it out except in the present indicative (ἐστίν is more often omitted than εἶ or εἰμί), and in the present
infinitive: see Schanz, Novae Commentationes Platonicae, p. 31 foll.

21. **ἐν αὐτοῖς διαβεβλημένος** = 'falsely accused to them' (Church). *ἐν* is here used as in Menex. 235 D ὅταν δέ τις ἐν τούτοις ἀγωνίζηται, οὕσπερ καὶ ἐπαινεῖ, i.e. it has reference to a court of law. With *αὐτοῖς* alone the phrase would mean 'at odds with them': πρὸς αὐτοὺς διαβεβλημένος would be 'calumniated to them'.

22. **εἰ γὰρ ὤφελον**: formula of wishing: Goodwin MT. 177. Compare our colloquial 'You *ought* to have been there'. *εἰ* in wishes is not to be explained by assuming an ellipse of the apodosis: it is more probable that *εἰ* in conditional sentences is a later use, derived from the use of εἰ = σϝει, cf. sei in Plautus and sī-c(e) to introduce a wish. See Monro's Homeric Grammar, p. 232 foll.

23. **ἵνα οἷοί τ' ἦσαν** = 'that they might have been able'. *ἵνα*, *ὅπως*, etc. are used with a secondary tense of the indicative (without *ἄν*) in final clauses depending on a wish that can no longer be realised, or on the apodosis to an impossible protasis: see Goodwin MT. p. 72. A similar rule holds for *πρίν* and *ἕως*: Goodwin 145, 144. Scribes frequently misunderstand the idiom and corrupt the text either (*a*) by inserting *ἄν*, or (*b*) by changing the indicatives to conjunctives or optatives: see Cobet, Variae Lectiones pp. 102, 359. Two passages, so far as I know, have not yet been emended. Marc. Aurelius, Book II. 11 τῶν δὲ λοιπῶν εἴ τι κακὸν ἦν, καὶ τοῦτο ἂν προείδοντο, ἵνα ἐπ' ᾖ πάντη τὸ μὴ περιπίπτειν αὐτῷ, where read ἐπῆν. The other is in Solon Frag. 36. 21 (κέντρον δ' ἄλλος ὡς ἐγὼ λαβὼν—οὔτ' ἂν κατέσχε δῆμον, οὔτ' ἐπαύσατο) πρὶν ἂν ταράξας πῖαρ ἐξέλη γάλα, where we should read ἀνταράξας and possibly ἐξεῖλεν, unless the corruption in ἐξέλη lies deeper[*].

24. **καὶ καλῶς ἂν εἶχεν**. Not of course dependent on *ἵνα*, as the *ἄν* shews, but an independent clause.

The statement that a power to do harm implies the power of doing good rests on the Socratic doctrine that virtue is knowledge. If we know what is good, we are good, but we cannot know what is good without knowing what is evil (this Socrates proved by the analogy of the arts), and so being able to do what is evil: conversely, the power to do evil implies the power to do good. This is all worked out at length in the Hippias Minor (a genuine dialogue), where it is proved that the veracious man is ὁ δυνάμενος ψεύδεσθαι: see especially 366 B foll. and 369 B (νῦν οὖν αἰσθάνει, ὅτι ἀναπέφανται ὁ αὐτὸς ὢν ψευδής τε καὶ ἀληθής), and compare Mem. IV. 2. 20.

---

[*] This correction has since been confirmed by the reading of the papyrus in Arist. Ἀθηναίων πολιτεία 12. 5.

νῦν δέ = 'but as it is': see on Apol. 18 A and Prot. 335 C (quoted there) ἀλλὰ σὲ ἐχρῆν ἡμῖν συγχωρεῖν—νῦν δὲ ἐπειδὴ οὐκ ἐθέλεις κτλ. The Latin is 'nunc'. οὐδέτερα in the next line is probably adverbial as in Theaet. 184 A (δεῖ δὲ οὐδέτερα i.e. neither ἐν παρέργῳ σκέψασθαι nor ἱκανῶς σκέψασθαι), although here it would be easy to supply ἐξεργάζεσθαι.

26. **ποιοῦσι δὲ τοῦτο ὅ τι ἄν τύχωσι** sc. ποιοῦντες. This does not mean 'they act wholly at random' (Church), as all the editors take it : had Plato meant that, he would have written πράττουσι as in Symp. 181 B ξυμβαίνει αὐτοῖς, ὅ τι ἄν τύχωσι, τοῦτο πράττειν. Supply τινὰ implied in φρόνιμον and ἄφρονα: the construction ποιεῖν τί τινα is quite usual: cf. infra 51 A. Translate: 'they treat a man just as it occurs to them'. Cf. Gorgias 521 C ἀνόητος ἄρα εἰμί, ὦ Καλλίκλεις, ὡς ἀληθῶς, εἰ μὴ οἴομαι ἐν τῇδε τῇ πόλει ὁντινοῦν ἄν ὅ τι τύχοι τοῦτο παθεῖν. Ibid. 522 C (which Stallbaum actually quotes to illustrate his view, as if πάσχειν could be a passive to πράττειν as well as to ποιεῖν !) ὥστε ἴσως, ὅ τι ἄν τύχω, τοῦτο πείσομαι. Socrates means that 'the many' are altogether thoughtless in their treatment of the individual: witness the way in which Miltiades, Cimon and Pericles were treated (Gorg. 515 E—516 E). They would lightly put a man to death and just as lightly bring him to life again if they could : see infra 48 C μὴ ὡς ἀληθῶς ταῦτα, ὦ Κρίτων, σκέμματα ᾖ τῶν ῥᾳδίως ἀποκτιννύντων καὶ ἀναβιωσκομένων γ' ἄν, εἰ οἷοί τ' ἦσαν, οὐδενὶ ξὺν νῷ, τούτων τῶν πολλῶν.

CHAPTER IV.

In this chapter Crito urges Socrates not to let the fear of danger to his friends or exile to himself prevent him from absconding.

44 E　　1. **μὲν δή.** This particle is regularly used to indicate that some topic is concluded. So at the end of speeches οἱ μὲν δὴ ταῦτα ἔλεγον, and the tragic τοιαῦτα μὲν δὴ ταῦτα. Note the contrast between ταῦτα retrospective and τάδε prospective.

2. **ἆρά γε μή.** ἆρα or ἆρά γε (the addition of γε makes the question more animated) merely indicates that a question is asked: ἆρα μή or ἆρά γε μή expects the answer 'no': ἆρά γε οὐ or ἆρ' οὐ expects the answer 'yes'. μή (μῶν) can of course stand by itself in the sense of num? as οὐ in the sense of nonne?

3. **προμηθεῖ—μή.** προμηθεῖσθαι being virtually a verb of fearing is followed by μή.

4. **οἱ συκοφά:ται** 'the informers'. The great part played by the law-courts and litigation in Athenian life caused a class of informers to spring up, resembling the 'delatores' of the early Roman empire. The origin of the name is obscure : see Liddell and Scott s. v., where a suggestion of Mr Lancelot Shadwell is quoted, according to which the word originally means 'one who brings figs to light by shaking the trees' : and then metaphorically 'one who makes rich men yield up their fruit by accusations and other vile arts' : cf. Antipho περὶ τοῦ χορευτοῦ § 43 ἔσειε καὶ ἐσυκοφάντει.

5. **πράγματα παρέχωσιν** of a prolonged action)(ἀναγκασθῶμεν of the act and nothing more.

6. **ἢ καὶ—ἢ—ἢ καί** = aut adeo—aut certe—aut etiam.

7. **ἀποβαλεῖν** is used both of voluntary and of involuntary !oss (as here) : cf. Symp. 179 A ὅπλα ἀποβαλών (voluntary) : Rep. VIII. 553 B τὴν οὐσίαν ἅπασαν ἀποβαλόντα (voluntary).

ἄλλο τι πρὸς τούτοις παθεῖν : euphemistic for death or exile.

9. **δίκαιοί ἐσμεν** = 'it is right that we'. The Greek idiom is 45 A personal while ours is impersonal. Goodwin MT. p. 195.

11. **μὴ ἄλλως ποίει** = 'do not say no'. **ἄλλως ποιεῖν** is an idiomatic expression = 'to refuse', 'to decline' : Symp. 173 E μὴ ἄλλως ποιήσῃς. Rep. I 328 B ἀλλὰ μένετε καὶ μὴ ἄλλως ποιεῖτε. Aristoph. Aves 133 καὶ μηδαμῶς ἄλλως ποιήσῃς. The expression does not seem to occur except in prohibitions or entreaties with μή : see Schanz, Novae Commentationes Platonicae p. 25.

12. **καὶ ταῦτα προμηθοῦμαι—πολλά.** Socrates lets the Laws reply infra 53 B.

14. **μήτε τοίνυν.** Note the effective balance : καὶ ταῦτα—καὶ ἄλλα πολλά, says Socrates : μήτε—ταῦτα—μήτε κτλ. says Crito. The second μήτε is in 45 B, line 24 : Crito's earnestness has an injurious effect upon his style : observe for example the recurrence of ἔπειτα within three lines just below. Wohlrab takes a somewhat different view : "Crito ut ipse hebetioris erat ingenii, ita oratio eius non nullis locis durior est minusque elegans".

καὶ γὰρ οὐδέ = neque enim.

15. **θέλουσι.** Even after a vowel Plato more frequently uses ἐθέλω than θέλω : yet Phaed. 77 C εἰ θέλετε : ibid. 115 B μὴ θέλητε : Symp. 190 D μὴ θέλωσιν : Schanz Nov. Comment. Plat. p. 102.

17. **τούτους τοὺς συκοφάντας.** τούτους = 'istos' expresses contempt : so very frequently in Greek : cf. Symp. 181 E τούτους τοὺς πανδήμους ἐραστάς. Our English 'your' is often used in the same way.

εὐτελεῖς = 'cheap': Crito contemptuously speaks of the informers as a commodity to be bought. We are told in the Memorabilia (II. 9) that Crito had himself suffered much from the συκοφάνται until following the advice of Socrates he engaged a vigorous but poor friend Archedemus to retaliate.

18. ἐπ᾽ αὐτούς = 'for them': there is much scorn in this phrase. ἐπί in this sense is regularly used of inanimate objects (ἐπ᾽ αὐτὸ τοῦτο line 22): the idea implied in εὐτελεῖς is therefore kept up.

σοὶ δὲ ὑπάρχει. σοί is emphatic)(ἐπ᾽ αὐτούς.

45 B   19. ὡς ἐγὼ οἶμαι ἱκανά. ὡς ἐγὼ οἶμαι and similar phrases generally precede the word or phrase which they modify: cf. infr. 46 D ὥσπερ νῦν δὴ ἐγὼ ἔλεγον ὅτι κτλ.: Gorg. 452 B ὡς ἐγῷμαι, πάνυ καταφρονῶν ἁπάντων, and ibid. 462 A.

ἔπειτα καὶ εἰ: καὶ goes with εἰ and not with ἔπειτα.

20. ἐμοῦ κηδόμενος: on account of the danger from the συκοφάνται, not of course for the loss of the money. Socrates did not think money a good nor the loss of it an evil, either in his own case or in that of his friends: see Apol. 38 B, where he proposes the penalty of 30 minae, to be paid by Plato and Crito and others.

ξένοι οὗτοι—ἀναλίσκειν. As ξένοι they would escape the συκοφάνται. The pronoun οὗτοι is deictic: 'see! here are foreigners ready to spend theirs'. Crito in his animation speaks as if the ξένοι were actually present in the prison: "de degentibus in urbe quosque fere quotidie videbat quasi de praesentibus loquitur Crito" (Buttmann). So in Symp. 175 A ἄλλον δέ τινα τῶν παίδων ἥκειν ἀγγέλλοντα ὅτι Σωκράτης οὗτος ἀναχωρήσας ἐν τῷ τῶν γειτόνων προθύρῳ ἕστηκεν: where Socrates is not as yet visible. ἐνθάδε means 'in Athens'. There is a certain awkwardness in the collocation οὗτοι ἐνθάδε (for οὗτοι implies ἐνθάδε): but it is not necessary to omit either of the two words. Crito is somewhat excited and prefers expressiveness to logic: see on 45 A line 14 above. The omission of the copula with ἕτοιμοι is common but not universal in Plato: contrast Prot. 313 B ἕτοιμος δ᾽ εἰ ἀναλίσκειν: see Schanz, Novae Comment. Plat. p. 35.

22. ἐπ᾽ αὐτὸ τοῦτο: see on line 18 (ἐπ᾽ αὐτούς) above.

Σιμμίας ὁ Θηβαῖος—Κέβης. Simmias and Cebes (who was also a Theban) play a prominent part in the discussion about immortality in the Phaedo. See Archer-Hind's edition of the dialogue pp. 40—42.

23. ἄλλοι πολλοὶ πάνυ. No doubt some or all of those named in Phaed. 59 B—C as present at the death of Socrates.

24. ὅπερ λέγω: viz. supra line 14. In such phrases the present is preferred to the past: see on ὅπερ λέγω Apol. 21 A.

ἀποκάμῃς. ἀποκάμνειν is to give over from weariness: cf. infra 45 D σὺ δέ μοι δοκεῖς τὰ ῥᾳθυμότατα αἱρεῖσθαι. Plato uses the verb sometimes absolutely (especially in phrases like Rep. IV. 435 D μὴ τοίνυν ἀποκάμῃς ἀλλὰ σκόπει: see Schanz, N. C. Pl. 25 note 2), sometimes with a participle: this seems to be the only passage where he has an infinitive following it, but cf. Eur. Ion 134—135 μοχθεῖν οὐκ ἀποκάμνω. Jacobs is here guilty of the solecism μὴ ἀποκνῇς, which is also printed by Schanz in his text.

25. ὃ ἔλεγες ἐν τῷ δικαστηρίῳ: Apol. 37 C—D.

δυσχερές σοι γενέσθω = 'trouble you'. It may have seemed little to Crito that Socrates should be false to what was said in the excitement of his defence when he himself was ready to break his deliberate promise to the Athenian people: see above on 44 C line 3. On μή with the 3rd person of the Aorist Imperative see Goodwin MT. 181.

26. οὐκ ἂν ἔχοις ἐξελθών κτλ. Apol. l. c. καλὸς οὖν ἄν μοι ὁ βίος εἴη ἐξελθόντι κτλ. This shews that ἐξελθών refers to quitting Athens, not to quitting the prison.

27. πολλαχοῦ—ἄλλοσε. We should expect ἄλλοθι: πολλαχόσε would not mend matters, since ἀγαπᾶν ποι is not Greek. The phrase is not strictly grammatical: καί = 'also', not 'and'. ἄλλοσε is of course attracted to the following relative, as in βῆναι κεῖθεν ὅθεν περ ἥκει in Soph. O. C. 1227.

28. εἰς Θετταλίαν. According to Diog. Laert. II. 5. 25 So- 45 C crates declined invitations from Scopas of Crannon and Eurylochus of Larissa. The story that he refused an invitation to the court of Archelaus (whither Euripides, Agathon, Zeuxis and others went) is better authenticated: see Arist. Rhet. III. 23. 1398ᵃ 24 Σωκράτης οὐκ ἔφη βαδίζειν ὡς Ἀρχέλαον· ὕβριν γὰρ ἔφη εἶναι τὸ μὴ δύνασθαι ἀμύνασθαι ὁμοίως εὖ παθόντα, ὥσπερ καὶ κακῶς. Crito's connection with Thessaly is significant as to his political sympathies: in so far as he felt any interest in politics, he favoured the καλοὶ κἀγαθοί or oligarchical party.

CHAPTER V.

Crito concludes his appeal to Socrates by urging that it is wrong to choose the more indolent course and remain to die: he ought to think of his children and his friends.

1. ἔτι δὲ οὐδὲ δίκαιον. With the form of expression compare Apol. 35 B (the concluding part of Socrates' appeal as this is of Crito's) χωρὶς δὲ τῆς δόξης, ὦ ἄνδρες, οὐδὲ δίκαιόν μοι δοκεῖ εἶναι κτλ. It is not correct to translate δίκαιον here as 'just': it is 'right', 'moral'. This is the original meaning of the word, and far more frequent than the other, i.e. just)(σώφρων, φρόνιμος, ἀνδρεῖος— the other three cardinal virtues. Aristotle recognises both meanings of the word: see Eth. v. 1129^b 25 where the pseudo-Theognic line ἐν δὲ δικαιοσύνῃ συλλήβδην πᾶσ' ἀρετὴ ἔνι (Bergk 147) is quoted to illustrate the wider meaning. It was this sense that Socrates assigned to the word when he declared τὸ δίκαιον to be identical with τὸ νόμιμον: see Mem. IV. 4. 12 and cf. Introd. p. xiii. This wider meaning survives in the English 'justify'.

2. ἐπιχειρεῖν πρᾶγμα. ἐπιχειρεῖν may take the accusative of a neuter noun denoting some inanimate object. Wohlrab compares Isocrates I. 3 καλὸν μὲν ἔργον ἐπιχειροῦσιν. σαυτὸν προδοῦναι is explanatory of πρᾶγμα, to which it stands in apposition.

3. καὶ τοιαῦτα σπεύδεις. There is more force and indignation in σπεύδεις than σπεύδειν would have conveyed.

Crito means that Socrates' defence was meaningless unless he regarded it as important that he should live. He had spoken of himself as God's minister to the Athenians: was he to desert his post because they rejected him? See Apol. Chapter XVIII.

5. σὲ διαφθεῖραι—"σέ is accented for emphasis, and to disconnect it from ἔσπευσαν". Dyer.

7. υἱεῖς. Socrates had three sons: Lamprocles and two others. Lamprocles was the eldest (Mem. II. 2. 1); but he was still a youth when Socrates died (Apol. 34 D): the other two were children (Apol. l. c. and Phaed. 116 B). We do not know whether they suffered in any way from their father's death. For the form υἱεῖς see my note on Apol. 20 A: the forms of the second declension (except υἱέος υἱεῖ as well as υἱοῦ υἱῷ) are preferred in the singular: those of the third in the dual and plural. Attic inscriptions of Plato's time more often omit the ι than not (ὑός ὑέος etc. See Meisterhans, Gram-

matik der Attischen Inschriften, p. 62): there are traces of the same omission in some MSS of Plato, and Schanz now everywhere writes the word without the ι (see his preface to the Laws p. VIII).

προδιδόναι=ἐπιχειρεῖν προδοῦναι, whence the present. So διδόναι often means 'to offer'.

8. ἐκθρέψαι καὶ ἐκπαιδεῦσαι: their τροφή and παιδεία was 45 D already begun: whence the preposition: cf. infra 50 E ἐξετράφης (Socrates was a grown man) καὶ ἐπαιδεύθης. τροφή is rather personal and moral surveillance than intellectual: παιδεία *vice versa*.

9. οἰχήσει καταλιπών='you will leave in the lurch'. The words imply that there would be something selfish and cowardly in the betrayal. τὸ σὸν μέρος =pro tua parte, quod ad te attinet (Cron): so infra 50 B.

ὅ τι ἂν τύχωσι (sc. πράττοντες) τοῦτο πράξουσι='they will have to fare as chance directs', 'they will have to take their chance in life': ὅ τι ἂν τύχωσι as in 44 D. With τοῦτο πράττειν cf. ἀγαθόν τι πράξοντες Alc. II. 141 D.

11. ἐν ταῖς ὀρφανίαις—ὀρφανούς. Göbel points out that the repetition of the idea has a pathetic effect.

12. ἢ γὰρ οὐ χρή...παιδεύοντα. Crito here pleads that one owes a duty to one's family as well as to the State: Socrates placed his duty to the State before his duty to his family. ποιεῖσθαι παῖδας i. q. παιδοποιεῖσθαι.

14. σὺ δέ μοι δοκεῖς τὰ ῥᾳθυμότατα αἱρεῖσθαι. I cannot but think that Crito contrasted the indifference of Socrates with the zeal displayed in his behalf by himself and the others: there is a touch of injured friendship about these words. See the reply of Socrates in 47 A (καὶ οὐκ ἂν σὲ παρακρούοι ἡ παροῦσα ξυμφορά) and my note there.

16. φάσκοντά γε δή=quippe qui dicat. The touch of sarcasm in φάσκοντα is made sharper by the addition of δή. For the assertion itself compare Apol. 30 A and 37 B. διὰ παντὸς τοῦ βίου has more force if taken with φάσκοντα than with ἐπιμελεῖσθαι.

17. ὡς ἔγωγε κτλ. χρὴ αἱρεῖσθαι being virtually an imperative may be followed by ὡς in the sense of 'for'.

18. μὴ δόξῃ. For αἰσχύνομαι followed by μή cf. Theaet. 183 E 45 E Μέλισσον—αἰσχυνόμενος μὴ φορτικῶς σκοπῶμεν.

19. ἀνανδρίᾳ τινὶ τῇ ἡμετέρᾳ. Here the taunt of cowardice (already implied in ῥᾳθυμότατα of 14 and ἀνὴρ ἀγαθὸς καὶ ἀνδρεῖος of 15) is openly made: for by ἡμετέρᾳ (as is clear from ὑπὲρ σοῦ in

17 and οὐδὲ σὺ σαυτόν in 25) Socrates is meant as well as Crito and his friends. It is implied that death requires less courage than life —a view which Socrates himself held. The reproach is made less biting by τινί.

20. **καὶ ἡ εἴσοδος—καὶ αὐτὸς ὁ ἀγὼν—καὶ τὸ τελευταῖον δὴ τουτὶ—δοκεῖν.** This explains in detail ἅπαν τὸ πρᾶγμα. There is clearly an allusion to the stage. The tragedy begins—(εἴσοδος) develops (αὐτὸς ὁ ἀγών)—and ends in a fiasco (ὥσπερ κατάγελως τῆς πράξεως): "solvuntur risu tabulae". The words are carefully chosen to suggest the comparison. εἴσοδος may be used both of the entrance of an actor (compare the use of εἰσάγειν in Apol. 35 B), and of the coming on of a law-suit (see on Apol. 24 D): ἀγών signifies 'acting' as well as 'pleading': the word always implies rivalry as well as publicity.

21. **εἰσῆλθες.** So I read with E and the second hand in B: the editors (except Stallbaum) generally read εἰσῆλθεν. The latter is very idiomatic Greek, for εἰσέρχομαι is used in this way as the passive to εἰσάγω: compare Dem. πρὸς Λάκριτον 49 ποῖ οὖν δεῖ ταύτην εἰσελθεῖν τὴν δίκην, but (see following note) εἰσῆλθες goes better with ἐξὸν μὴ εἰσελθεῖν: cf. also on 45 E infra κακίᾳ τινὶ—δοκεῖν.

ἐξὸν (sc. σοι) μὴ εἰσελθεῖν. Crito probably means that Socrates might have effected his escape in the interval between the lodging of the indictment with the King Archon and the actual trial. Had he done so, the case would have been decided against him by default, see on ἐρήμην κατηγοροῦντες Apol. 18 C. If we read ὡς εἰσῆλθεν and not ὡς εἰσῆλθες, we must understand αὐτῇ i.e. τῇ δίκῃ after ἐξόν: this can hardly be right, for even if Socrates had absconded the trial would have come on: the only difference would have been the absence of the defendant. There is no good authority for the tradition that Anytus wished to make terms with Socrates after the indictment had been lodged; nor would such a course have been tolerated by Athenian law, since ἀσέβεια was a γραφή or offence against the State, not a δίκη or lawsuit with a private individual.

22. **τὸ τελευταῖον δὴ τουτί** = 'last of all this present scene': the περιπέτεια as it were or catastrophe of the tragedy. The Bodleian has δήπου.

23. **ὥσπερ κατάγελως τῆς πράξεως** = 'a *reductio ad absurdum* as one might say of the whole affair'. τῆς πράξεως is an objective genitive: cf. Aesch. Ag. 1264 τί δῆτ', ἐμαυτῆς καταγέλωτ', ἔχω τάδε καὶ σκῆπτρα καὶ μαντεῖα περὶ δέρῃ στέφη; See the retort of the

Laws infra 53 D ἴσως ἂν ἡδέως σου ἀκούοιεν ὡς γελοίως ἐκ τοῦ δεσμωτηρίου ἀπεδίδρασκες κτλ. On κατάγελως (καταγέλαστον) see infra 53 A.

κακίᾳ τινὶ—δοκεῖν = 'that you should be thought to have given
us the slip, through a sort of cowardice and unmanliness on our
part'. δοκεῖν διαπεφευγέναι is explanatory of τουτί, exactly as σαυτὸν
προδοῦναι is of πρᾶγμα in 45 C line 2. The subject to δοκεῖν is σε:
this is easily supplied from the context (τὸ πρᾶγμα τὸ περὶ σέ in 19
and ὡς εἰσῆλθες in 21). For the expression compare Phaed. 115 C
ἐάνπερ γε λάβητέ με καὶ μὴ ἐκφύγω ὑμᾶς, and for διαφεύγω compare
Hipp. Major 294 E βαβαί, οἴχεται ἄρα ἡμᾶς διαπεφευγός, ὦ Ἱππία.
Göbel takes ἡμᾶς as subject to δοκεῖν: Wohlrab τὸ τελευταῖον
δὴ τουτί: the other editors fail to give any clear explanation of this
difficult passage. There is some awkwardness in having δοκεῖν διαπεφευγέναι as virtually a subject to δόξῃ in line 18 above: but the
grammatical subject is τουτί, to which δοκεῖν is in apposition. Mudge
conjectures δοκῇ, but the text is quite sound.

25. **οὐδὲ σὺ σαυτόν.** The relative clause passes into a main 46 A
sentence as in Xen. Anab. 1. 4. 9 ἰχθύων—οὓς οἱ Σύροι θεοὺς ἐνόμιζον,
καὶ ἀδικεῖν οὐκ εἴων, οὐδὲ τὰς περιστεράς: compare also Gorg. 452 D
τί ἐστι τοῦτο ὃ φῂς σὺ μέγιστον ἀγαθὸν εἶναι—καὶ σὲ δημιουργὸν εἶναι
αὐτοῦ, and see my note on Apol. 40 A ἅ γε δὴ οἰηθείη—καὶ νομίζεται.

οἷόν τε ὂν καὶ δυνατόν. The twofold expression is for emphasis:
cf. infra line 31 ἀδύνατον καὶ οὐκέτι οἷόν τε. οἷόν τε is 'feasible':
δυνατόν 'possible'.

27. **ἅμα τῷ κακῷ.** ἅμα is used in much the same way as πρός:
τῷ κακῷ is substantival. So in the Gorgias (474 E foll.) τὸ αἰσχρόν
is defined as that which is at once λυπηρόν τε καὶ κακόν: see also 475 B
οὐκοῦν εἴπερ αἴσχιον τὸ ἀδικεῖν τοῦ ἀδικεῖσθαι, ἤτοι λυπηρότερόν ἐστι
καὶ λύπῃ ὑπερβάλλον αἴσχιον ἂν εἴη ἢ κακῷ ἢ ἀμφοτέροις;

28. **μᾶλλον δέ** = vel potius, as in Gorg. 449 A μᾶλλον δέ, ὦ
Γοργία, αὐτὸς ἡμῖν εἰπέ. οὐδέ is ne—quidem.

29. **βουλεύεσθαι)(βεβουλεῦσθαι.** "Charm. 176 C οὗτοι, ἦν δ'
ἐγώ, τί βουλεύεσθον ποιεῖν; οὐδέν, ἔφη ὁ Χαρμίδης, ἀλλὰ βεβου-
λεύμεθα." Jacobs. Note the fourfold recurrence of βουλεύεσθαι
(βουλή).

30. **τῆς γὰρ ἐπιούσης νυκτός.** Apparently Crito does not believe the vision (see on 44 B above): the γυνὴ καλὴ καὶ εὐειδής left
Socrates one night more in which to effect his escape. With τῆς
ἐπιούσης νυκτός cf. τῆς ἐπιούσης ἡμέρας in 44 A.

33. **μηδαμῶς ἄλλως ποίει:** see on 45 A μὴ ἄλλως ποίει.

CHAPTER VI.

Crito's pleading is now concluded. In reply, Socrates begins by laying down the principles which should guide his decision. He first recalls one great doctrine on which he had insisted throughout all his life, viz. that no opinions are worth regarding except the opinions of those who know. See Introduction pp. xi and xii.

46 B   2. **πολλοῦ ἀξία** sc. ἐστίν, although εἰ—εἴη follows: a "mixed conditional sentence" Goodwin MT. 118. It would not be possible to understand ἂν εἴη: if the optative of the copula is omitted in an apodosis with ἄν, the ἄν must be inserted: see Meno 96 B οὐκοῦν εἰ μήτε οἱ σοφισταὶ μήτε οἱ αὐτοὶ καλοὶ κἀγαθοὶ ὄντες διδάσκαλοί εἰσι τοῦ πράγματος, δῆλον, ὅτι οὐκ ἂν ἄλλοι γε ; But even apart from this, in cases like the present Greek prefers the more dogmatic form of expression. Note εἰ—εἴη and not εἰ—ἦν: Socrates speaks as one who has not yet made up his mind—ready to follow ὅπῃ ἂν ὁ λόγος ὥσπερ πνεῦμα φέρῃ (Rep. III. 394 D).

4. **σκοπεῖσθαι** is placed in the emphatic position at the beginning of the sentence as if=σκοπεῖσθαι ἀλλὰ μὴ προθυμεῖσθαι.

5. **οὐ μόνον νῦν.** So the MSS: there is no reason to read οὐ νῦν πρῶτον with Nauck and Schanz. The omission of the copula is not very common in Plato except when it is ἐστίν: yet cf. Prot. 335 C ἐγὼ δὲ τὰ μακρὰ ταῦτα ἀδύνατος = Theaet. 169 B ἰσχυρικώτερος μέντοι ἐγὼ ἐκείνων. εἰ and ἐσμέν are also sometimes omitted : ἦν rarely, except in the phrase εἰ μὴ διά τινα (σέ or the like): parts of the conjunctive and optative are very seldom omitted : εἶναι however is left out very frequently. See Schanz, Novae Comm. Pl. 31—35.

6. **τῶν ἐμῶν μηδενὶ ἄλλῳ πείθεσθαι.** This is the reply to Crito's πείθου μοι (46 A), for τῶν ἐμῶν includes Socrates' friends as well as everything else that could be called his.

7. **ἢ τῷ λόγῳ—φαίνηται.** A faithful description of Socrates' rule of life. For example, before entering on a line of conduct he would inquire if it harmonised with the conception or definition (λόγος) of τὸ δίκαιον which he had arrived at by the exercise of his reason : and if it did, nothing ever deterred him from so acting : see my Introduction to the Apology p. xi; compare also Phaed. 100 A, where Plato uses the phraseology of the Socratic method to describe his own procedure ὑποθέμενος ἑκάστοτε λόγον ὃν ἂν κρίνω ἐρρωμενέστατον εἶναι, ἃ μὲν ἄν μοι δοκῇ τούτῳ συμφωνεῖν, τίθημι

ὡς ἀληθῆ ὄντα—ἃ δ' ἂν μή, ὡς οὐκ ἀληθῆ. See also Euthyphr.
6 E ταύτην τοίνυν με αὐτὴν δίδαξον τὴν ἰδέαν, τίς ποτέ ἐστιν, ἵνα εἰς
ἐκείνην ἀποβλέπων καὶ χρώμενος αὐτῇ παραδείγματι, ὃ μὲν ἂν
τοιοῦτον ᾖ, ὧν ἂν ἢ σὺ ἢ ἄλλος τις πράττῃ, φῶ ὅσιον εἶναι, ὃ δ' ἂν μὴ
τοιοῦτον, μὴ φῶ : and compare as to this point Dr Jackson on the
"incomplete Protagoreans" of the Theaetetus in Journal of Philo-
logy, Vol. XIII. 249—250.

9. **ἔλεγον** : imperfect, because Socrates is referring to the
teaching of his whole life. Infra ἐκβαλεῖν = 'throw over', 'discard',
as in Rep. VI. 503 A τὸ δόγμα τοῦτο μήτ' ἐν πόνοις μήτ' ἐν φό-
βοις μήτ' ἐν ἄλλῃ μηδεμιᾷ μεταβολῇ φαίνεσθαι ἐκβάλλοντας. μοι
γέγονεν is 'has come to me': cf. Euthyphr. 3 B σὺ τὸ δαιμόνιον φῄς
σαυτῷ ἑκάστοτε γίγνεσθαι.

10. **ὅμοιοι** (sc. λόγοι) is probably the subject and not the predicate, otherwise in place of ἐκβαλεῖν we should expect a word
= 'to change': the predicate is φαίνονται (sc. βέλτιστοι). ὅμοιοι is
not = οἱ αὐτοί (idem) but = Latin similes: the two ideas are carefully distinguished in Theaet. 159 A εἰ ἄρα τι συμβαίνει ὅμοιόν τῳ
γίγνεσθαι ἢ ἀνόμοιον—ὁμοιούμενον μὲν ταὐτὸν φήσομεν γίγνεσθαι, ἀνομοιούμενον δὲ ἕτερον; ἀνάγκη. Socrates becomes
more confident as he goes on: σχεδόν τι ὅμοιοι—καὶ τοὺς αὐτοὺς
πρεσβεύω κτλ.

11. **πρεσβεύω** is a lofty and somewhat poetic word, frequently 46 C
used of regard paid to the gods.

12. **βελτίω ἔχωμεν λέγειν** = βελτίους ἔχωμεν λόγους.

13. **οὐ μή σοι ξυγχωρήσω** : see on 44 B οὐδένα μή ποτε εὑρήσω.
οὐδ' ἂν πλείω—μορμολύττηται : πλείω is adverbial like ἐλάττω
in Rep. 396 D ἐλάττω δὲ καὶ ἧττον—ἐσφαλμένον : cf. also infra
53 A ἐλάττω ἐξ αὐτῆς ἀπεδήμησας. The Μορμώ was well known
in the Greek nursery (see Theocr. XV. 40 οὐκ ἀξῶ τυ, τέκνον. Μορμώ
—δάκνει ἵππος). Other bogies were Ἀκκώ, Ἀλφιτώ, Λαμία, Γοργώ,
Μορμολύκη, Ἔμπουσα: see Becker's Charicles E. T. pp. 224—
225. Compare the well-known passage in the Phaedo (77 E) ἀλλ'
ἴσως ἔνι τις καὶ ἐν ἡμῖν παῖς, ὅστις τὰ τοιαῦτα φοβεῖται· τοῦτον
οὖν πειρώμεθα πείθειν μὴ δεδιέναι τὸν θάνατον ὥσπερ τὰ μορμο-
λύκεια.

It should be noted that the order of the words ὥσπερ παῖδας
ἡμᾶς is very idiomatic: the effect is almost to identify the objects
compared. If ἡμᾶς preceded ὥσπερ παῖδας the connection between
the two would be much less close. Still more idiomatic is the

construction in similes with ὥσπερ and a preposition. If it is
wished to bring the objects compared into the closest possible
union, ὥσπερ (ὡς) with the preposition is placed first, and the preposition itself written only once : see for example Rep. VIII. 545 E
ὡς πρὸς παῖδας ἡμᾶς παιζούσας καὶ ἐρεσχηλούσας, Theaet. 170 A
ὥσπερ πρὸς θεοὺς ἔχειν τοὺς ἐν ἑκάσταις ἄρχοντας. Manuscripts however often violate the rule so far as the omission of the
preposition is concerned : see Cobet, Variae Lectiones p. 165 foll.

15. δεσμοὺς καὶ θανάτους κτλ. δεσμοί = chains) (δεσμά = imprisonment : see on Apol. 32 C. The plural (δεσμοί, θάνατοι, χρημάτων ἀφαιρέσεις) adds to the rhetorical effect : the many have a variety
of deaths etc., from which to choose our μορμώ.

16. ἐπιπέμπουσα : compare Phaed. 62 C πρὶν ἂν ἀνάγκην τινὰ
θεὸς ἐπιπέμψῃ. The word means 'inflicting on' (Church), not of
course 'threatening with'. Socrates means that death is only a μορμώ,
not simply in the anticipation but in the actual suffering of it. Dr
Verrall suggests ἐπέμπουσα as if = 'assuming the forms of' like
the Empusa. I am far from satisfied that ἐπέμπουσα is rightly
formed, nor even allowing this does the construction seem quite
natural : but I think that Plato may have written ἐπιπέμπουσα
rather than ἐπιφέρουσα let us say, because the ending is identical
with ἔμπουσα : see my note on 47 B line 14 for more examples of
the play upon words in Plato.

17. αὐτά = 'the question' : see on 44 C ἡγήσονται αὐτὰ οὕτω
πεπρᾶχθαι.

πρῶτον μέν : repeated infra 48 A (ὥστε πρῶτον μὲν ταύτῃ οὐκ
ὀρθῶς εἰσηγεῖ), where the first inquiry is concluded : the second point
is then raised by way of protest against the first (ibid. ἀλλὰ μὲν δή,
φαίη γ' ἄν τις, οἵοί τέ εἰσιν ἡμᾶς οἱ πολλοὶ ἀποκτινύναι) : hence πρῶτον
μέν has no εἶτα or εἶτα δέ to balance it.

18. τοῦτον τὸν λόγον ἀναλάβοιμεν = 'recur to this view' : οὗτος
is often = 'that of yours', here made clearer by ὃν σὺ λέγεις. ἀναλαμ-
βάνω is 'iterum sumo'—'take up where I laid down' as in Rep. VI.
490 D πάλιν ἀνειλήφαμεν τὴν τῶν ἀληθῶς φιλοσόφων φύσιν. The
reference is to 44 B—D, and 45 E.

19. πότερον καλῶς ἐλέγετο κτλ. This depends on ἀναλάβοιμεν :
cf. Apol. 19 A ἀναλάβωμεν οὖν ἐξ ἀρχῆς τίς ἡ κατηγορία ἐστίν ; In
English we must say 'recur—and ask if'. The subject to ἐλέγετο is
ὁ λόγος, to be understood from τοῦτον τὸν λόγον : it is defined by the
clause ὅτι ταῖς μὲν—οὔ. The imperfect is used because Socrates

refers to the teaching of his whole life, see on ἔλεγον in line 9 above. ἑκάστοτε means on every occasion when the subject was discussed. If there was one thing on which Socrates insisted more than any other, it was that no man's opinion is worth anything on any subject which he has not studied: see Grote Vol. VIII. p. 239 foll.

20. **ἢ πρὶν μὲν ἐμέ κτλ.** Three alternatives: either (*a*) the 46 D doctrine that only some δόξαι are worthy of regard was right, or (*b*) it was wrong, or (*c*) it was right then and wrong now. In his statement of the third alternative Socrates substitutes the application for the statement of the general principle—was *I* right in thinking it my duty to *die* then, although others thought otherwise, and am I wrong now?

21. **ἐμὲ δεῖν ἀποθνήσκειν.** Apol. 40 B κινδυνεύει γάρ μοι τὸ ξυμβεβηκὸς τοῦτο ἀγαθὸν γεγονέναι: and Socrates must often have said the same in declining Crito's former invitations to escape: see on 44 B ἔτι καὶ νῦν ἐμοὶ πείθου καὶ σώθητι.

22. **κατάδηλος ἄρα:** i.e. of course ὁ λόγος: with δῆλος as with δίκαιος Greek prefers the personal mode of expression. ἄρα='after all' expresses surprise and disappointment. See on Apol. 34 c ἐγὼ δὲ οὐδὲν ἄρα τούτων ποιήσω.

ἄλλως [ἕνεκα λόγου]. I believe ἕνεκα λόγου to be a gloss on ἄλλως: the expression (ὁ λόγος) ἄλλως ἕνεκα λόγου is excessively awkward. For ἄλλως used in this way (='otherwise than it ought' i.e. nearly = εἰκῇ temere) cf. Phaed. 76 E ἄλλως ἂν ὁ λόγος οὗτος εἰρημένος εἴη, and the adverbial expression τὴν ἄλλως, as in Theaet. 172 E οἱ ἀγῶνες οὐδέποτε τὴν ἄλλως ἀλλ' ἀεὶ τὴν περὶ αὐτοῦ.

23. **ὡς ἀληθῶς.** Like τῷ ὄντι and τῇ ἀληθείᾳ this expression is frequent in the dialogues of Plato's early and middle period: in the later dialogues ἀληθῶς, ὄντως and ἀληθείᾳ (less frequent) are more common: see Schanz in Hermes (1886) XXI. 3, pp. 439—459. As for the origin of the phrase, Schanz accepts the explanation given by Fox, according to whom ὡς is the ablative of the article, as ἀληθῶς is of ἀληθές: but surely τώς and not ὡς is the ablative of τό. The old explanation (which I prefer) is to regard the phrase as parallel to ὡς ἑτέρως, ὡς ἄλλως etc., and due to attraction like θαυμασίως ὡς: ἄνδρες σοφοὶ ὡς ἀληθῶς (Phaed. 63 A) for example is short for σοφοὶ οὕτως, ὡς ἀληθές ἐστιν. Kühner's Ausführliche Grammatik II. p. 921.

24. **ἐπισκέψασθαι κοινῇ μετὰ σοῦ.** κοινῇ σκοπεῖν, κοινῇ ζητεῖν etc. were almost technical terms of the Socratic dialectic: see Introd. to Apol. p. xv.

25. ἀλλοιότερος, like ὁ αὐτός, is in the predicate.

27. τῶν οἰομένων τι λέγειν. Socrates means himself primarily: but he chooses a phrase which will include Crito too, so as to make his conclusion appear as the verdict of all right-minded men. λέγειν τι)(οὐδὲν λέγειν, 'to be right')('to be wrong': so in English 'there is something in what you say'. So τὶ ποιεῖν = 'to be making something of it' in Symp. 173 A. ὧδε before ὑπὸ τῶν οἰομένων refers forward to ὅτι τῶν δοξῶν—τὰς δὲ μή.

28. ὥσπερ νῦν δὴ ἔλεγον goes with the following clause: in Eng. 'that as I said just now': see on 45 B ὡς ἐγὼ οἶμαι ἱκανά. νῦν δή = ἀρτίως as so often (see my note on Apol. 37 C): Cobet would write νυνδή, and Schanz now follows him: B too has νυνδὴ here. There is no special force in the imperfect: ἔλεγον and ἔφην (like ἐκέλευον in Phaed. 59 E and Phaedr. 228 B) are sometimes used as aorists. See also Goodwin MT. 8.

τῶν δοξῶν ἃς—δοξάζουσιν...τὰς δὲ μή: contrast this with 46 C lines 19—20. The principle is enunciated more precisely because upon it hinges the argument down to 48 A.

46 E   30. πρὸς θεῶν: only in entreaties, not in asseverations: Apol. 25 C.

31. ὅσα γε τἀνθρώπεια = 'in all human probability': for ὅσα γε cf. infr. 54 D ὅσα γε τὰ νῦν ἐμοὶ δοκοῦντα.

ἐκτὸς εἰ τοῦ μέλλειν—αὔριον. Why αὔριον? It is certain that Socrates believed that he would die upon the *third* day, but as Crito disbelieved the vision (see on 46 A) Socrates waives the point for the present. μέλλειν ἀποθνήσκειν = ἀποθανεῖσθαι.

47 A   33. παρακρούοι. Like σφάλλειν this word is probably a metaphor from the palaestra: cf. Theaet. 168 A τὰ σφάλματα ἃ αὐτὸς ὑφ' ἑαυτοῦ καὶ τῶν προτέρων συνουσιῶν παρεκέκρουστο. The original meaning may have been to give an unfair blow, hit below the belt. There is a touch of irony in οὐκ ἂν σὲ παρακρούοι: Socrates knew well that it was Crito and not he whose mental vision was dimmed by the coming doom (see Phaed. 84 E). I think the words are meant as a reply to Crito's taunt in 45 D σὺ δέ μοι δοκεῖς τὰ ῥᾳθυμότατα αἱρεῖσθαι, where σὺ is emphatic: see note. For this reason I have printed σὲ with an accent.

34. οὐχ ἱκανῶς: infra οὐχὶ καλῶς in line 36 is stronger: cf. in 46 B the change from ὅμοιοι to τοὺς αὐτούς: see note in loc. Hirschig's οὐχὶ καλῶς (the one tolerable suggestion of the thirty odd

suggestions which he has made on the Crito) completely misses the point.

36. **ἀλλὰ τὰς μέν, τὰς δ' οὔ**; After these words some inferior MSS (and the second hand in B) read οὐδὲ πάντων, ἀλλὰ τῶν μέν, τῶν δ' οὔ; Apart from their slender MS authority, the words are objectionable (a) because they correspond to nothing either in 46 C (ταῖς μὲν δεῖ τῶν δοξῶν προσέχειν τὸν νοῦν, ταῖς δὲ οὔ), or in 46 D (τῶν δοξῶν ἃς οἱ ἄνθρωποι δοξάζουσιν κτλ.), and (β) because they anticipate line 42 χρησταὶ δὲ οὐχ αἱ τῶν φρονίμων, πονηραὶ δὲ αἱ τῶν ἀφρόνων; Plato is especially careful to avoid any premature indications of the course of an argument: he professes to follow ὅπῃ ἂν ὁ λόγος ὥσπερ πνεῦμα φέρῃ (Rep. III. 394 D).

CHAPTER VII.

In this chapter Socrates recalls the familiar illustrations by which he used to enforce the doctrine that no opinion deserves to be considered except that of those who know, and applies them to the case in point. Introduction p. xii.

1. **τὰ τοιαῦτα ἐλέγετο**. τοιαῦτα refers to what follows: so in Rep. VI. 488 A νόησον γὰρ τοιουτονὶ γενόμενον εἴτε πολλῶν νεῶν πέρι εἴτε μιᾶς. It is a mistaken idea that τοιόσδε is invariably prospective, and τοιοῦτος retrospective. The imperfect ἐλέγετο is used because Socrates is recalling the doctrines taught throughout his life: see on ἔλεγον in 46 B.

2. **γυμναζόμενος ἀνήρ κτλ.** For the asyndeton cf. Rep. l. c. 47 B ναύκληρον μεγέθει μὲν καὶ ῥώμῃ ὑπὲρ τοὺς ἐν τῇ νηῒ πάντας, and Apol. 22 A (where see note) ἦ μὴν ἐγὼ ἔπαθόν τι τοιοῦτον· οἱ μὲν μάλιστα κτλ.

καὶ τοῦτο πράττων = 'and making this his work': hoc agens. Buttmann compares Xen. Hell. IV. 8. 22 οὐδὲ γὰρ ἐκράτουν αὐτοῦ αἱ τοῦ σώματος ἡδοναί, ἀλλ' ἀεί, πρὸς ᾧ εἴη ἔργῳ, τοῦτ' ἔπραττεν. Compare πρᾶγμα = 'profession' in Apol. 20 C.

5. **ἰατρὸς ἢ παιδοτρίβης**: see Gorg. 452 A foll. The ἰατρός is there regarded as the δημιουργὸς ὑγιείας: the παιδοτρίβης as the man whose ἔργον is καλούς τε καὶ ἰσχυροὺς ποιεῖν τοὺς ἀνθρώπους τὰ σώματα: and so Soph. 228 E περὶ μὲν αἶσχος γυμναστική, περὶ δὲ νόσον ἰατρική; φαίνεσθον. In another passage of the Gorgias (464 B foll.) ἰατρική and γυμναστική are described as the two

branches of the art which looks after the body (ἡ τοῦ σώματος θεραπεία); they are correlative (ἀντίστροφοι) with δικαιοσύνη (δικαστική) and νομοθετική, the two subdivisions of πολιτική or the art which pays attention to the soul. Plato frequently places the two professions side by side: e.g. Prot. 313 D ἐὰν μή τις τύχῃ γυμναστικὸς ἢ ἰατρὸς ὤν: Polit. 295 C et al. Cron remarks that both professions were united in the person of Herodicus of Selymbria: compare Rep. III. 406 B ʽΗρόδικος δὲ παιδοτρίβης ὢν καὶ νοσώδης γενόμενος, μίξας γυμναστικὴν ἰατρικῇ, ἀπέκναισε πρῶτον μὲν καὶ μάλιστα ἑαυτόν, ἔπειτ' ἄλλους ὕστερον πολλούς.

9. **ἀλλὰ μή**: ἀλλὰ is regular in such antitheses: see on Apol. 23 D.

12. **ταύτῃ—ᾗ ἂν κτλ.** Note the position of ταύτῃ: it serves to throw special emphasis on the clause introduced by ᾗ ἄν.

καὶ γυμναστέον καὶ ἐδεστέον γε καὶ ποτέον: this explains πρακτέον. In ἐδεστέον γε the γε is added because what follows inculcates obedience to the ἰατρός as γυμναστέον to the παιδοτρίβης: καὶ—γε is frequently used in this way to introduce something which belongs to a different class from the things already enumerated. Gorg. 450 D ἀριθμητικὴ καὶ λογιστικὴ καὶ γεωμετρικὴ καὶ πεττευτική γε καὶ ἄλλαι πολλαὶ τέχναι: here the first three arts hang together, being all concerned with number or mathematics. On the food of a Greek athlete cf. Aristotle Eth. Nic. II. 1106ᵃ 36 ff. οὐ γὰρ εἴ τῳ δέκα μναῖ (a mina was about 15·2 oz. Troy) φαγεῖν πολύ, δύο δὲ ὀλίγον, ὁ ἀλείπτης ἐξ μνᾶς προστάξει· ἔστι γὰρ ἴσως καὶ τοῦτο πολὺ τῷ ληψομένῳ ἢ ὀλίγον· Μίλωνι μὲν γὰρ ὀλίγον, τῷ δὲ ἀρχομένῳ τῶν γυμνασίων πολύ.

13. **τῷ ἐπιστάτῃ καὶ ἐπαΐοντι.** The argument gains additional point if it is noted that the word ἐπιστάτης suggests ἐπίσταμαι and so leads up to ἐπαΐοντι: Socrates wishes to deduce from the example of training the general principle that only he who knows deserves to be regarded. The word ἐπιστάτης is sometimes used in the sense of a trainer: cf. Xen. Mem. III. 5. 18 ἐν τοῖς γυμνικοῖς ἀγῶσι πείθονται τοῖς ἐπιστάταις (=paedotribis, as Schneider correctly explains it), and see also Rep. VII. 521 E σώματος γὰρ αὔξης καὶ φθίσεως ἐπιστατεῖ (sc. γυμναστική). Plato repeatedly thinks of ἐπίσταμαι when he uses the words ἐπιστάτης or ἐπιστατῶ: see for example Prot. 312 D foll. εἰ δέ τις ἐκεῖνο ἔροιτο· ὁ δὲ σοφιστὴς τῶν τί σοφῶν ἐστι; τί ἂν ἀποκριναίμεθα αὐτῷ; ποίας ἐργασίας ἐπιστάτης; τί ἂν εἴποιμεν αὐτὸν εἶναι—ἢ ἐπιστάτην τοῦ ποιῆσαι δεινὸν

λέγειν;—ὁ δὲ δὴ σοφιστὴς περὶ τίνος δεινὸν ποιεῖ λέγειν; ἢ δῆλον ὅτι περὶ οὗπερ καὶ ἐπίσταται; cf. Crat. 414 E τὸν σοφὸν ἐπιστάτην, and 390 B ἆρ' οὐχ οὗτος ὃς ἐπίσταιτο ἂν ἐργαζομένῳ κάλλιστα ἐπιστατεῖν: Rep. IV. 443 E σοφίαν δὲ τὴν ἐπιστατοῦσαν ταύτῃ τῇ πράξει ἐπιστήμην. I have no doubt that Socrates thought it a real confirmation of his view that knowledge should everywhere hold rule when he found that ἐπιστάτης and ἐπίσταμαι seem to be connected, and I think Plato hints at this in such passages as Polit. 311 C ὁπόταν—ἄρχῃ τε καὶ ἐπιστατῇ. 'God and Nature do nothing in vain': even the similarity of names is not without its significance: hence Plato wrote the Cratylus. A precisely similar phenomenon appears in the case of the word εὖ πράττειν. Just as here ἐπιστάτῃ forms the transition to ἐπαΐοντι, so in Charm. 173 D εὖ ἂν πράττοιμεν is the link between ἐπιστημόνως ἂν πράττοιμεν and εὐδαιμονοῖμεν (ἐπιστημόνως ἂν πράττοντες εὖ ἂν πράττοιμεν καὶ εὐδαιμονοῖμεν): see also 172 A and Alcibiades I. 116 B and compare Aristotle Eth. Nic. I. 1098^{b} 20 συνᾴδει δὲ τῷ λόγῳ καὶ τὸ εὖ ζῆν καὶ εὖ πράττειν τὸν εὐδαίμονα. So also in Phaed. 99 C δέον (which has two meanings) forms the link between ἀγαθόν and ξυνδεῖν—καὶ ὡς ἀληθῶς τὸ ἀγαθὸν καὶ δέον ξυνδεῖν καὶ ξυνέχειν: where it should be noted that the omission of the article before δέον (as here before ἐπαΐοντι) favours my view. Similarly in Symp. 204 C, where Plato proves that τὸ ἐρώμενον is καλὸν by means of the middle term ἐραστόν ('lovely' as well as 'loved'): καὶ γὰρ ἔστι τὸ ἐραστὸν τὸ τῷ ὄντι καλὸν κτλ.: the entire passage from 203 A to 204 D is full of such double meanings and constructions. See also Symp. 196 C. This sort of chain-inference (incorrectly called Sorites) was afterwards very popular in the Stoic school: see Reid on Cic. Acad. Pr. 49.

I have insisted on this point partly because the editors have ignored it and partly on account of the light it throws on the meaning of the vision in 44 B: Socrates was greatly influenced by similarity of name.

It should be noted that ἐπαΐειν is a favourite word of Plato's, but less common in other authors. Protagoras used the word frequently: according to Kock on Arist. Nubes 650 it was probably an importation from the Ionian philosophical schools into the sophistic and philosophical circles of Athens.

17. εἶεν was pronounced εἶέν with intervocalic aspiration as in ταώς: the derivation is doubtful, but it can hardly come from εἰμί:

see on Apol. 18 E. Possibly it is connected with εἶα: for as Timaeus s. v. says, it is not only συγκατάθεσις τῶν εἰρημένων, but also συναφὴ πρὸς τὰ μέλλοντα: whence Suidas explains it as = ἄγε δή. Here for example it leads up to ἀπειθήσας δὲ κτλ.: cf. Symp. 204 C εἶεν δή, ὦ ξένη· καλῶς γὰρ λέγεις· (parenthetical) τοιοῦτος ὢν ὁ Ἔρως τίνα χρείαν ἔχει τοῖς ἀνθρώποις;

47 C 18. **τὴν δόξαν καὶ τοὺς ἐπαίνους—τοὺς τῶν πολλῶν λόγους**: so all the best MSS. The difficulties felt with regard to the text arise from a misapprehension of the argument. Socrates is gradually passing from the illustration to the case which it was intended to illustrate. Hence at first when he is only elucidating the illustration he introduces more detail: supra 47 B φοβεῖσθαι χρὴ τοὺς ψόγους καὶ ἀσπάζεσθαι τοὺς ἐπαίνους: as the application draws near there is somewhat less detail (ἀτιμάσας τὴν δόξαν καὶ τοὺς ἐπαίνους): when we are on the verge of the application, there is only τιμήσας τοὺς τῶν πολλῶν λόγους, because it is a λόγος τῶν πολλῶν which all this was meant to illustrate, viz. that Crito and his friends and Socrates himself are cowards in leaving Socrates to die. Schanz brackets and Kral omits καὶ τοὺς ἐπαίνους: the other editors rightly retain the words. Ziwsa in the Zeitschr. f. d. öst. Gymn. 1879 p. 106 reads ἀπειθήσας δὲ τῷ ἑνὶ καὶ ἀτιμάσας αὐτοῦ τὴν δόξαν καὶ τοὺς ψόγους, τιμήσας δὲ τοὺς τῶν πολλῶν ἐπαίνους.

22. **ποῖ τείνει**: ποῖ = εἰς τί. Infra εἰς τί τῶν τοῦ ἀπειθοῦντός is like 46 B τῶν ἐμῶν μηδενὶ ἄλλῳ.

25. **οὐκοῦν καὶ τἄλλα—οὕτως**: "verbo omisso, ut Lach. 181 A εὖ γε νὴ τὴν Ἥραν—ὅτι ὀρθοῖς τὸν πατέρα". Wohlrab.

26. **καὶ δὴ καί** is used to introduce a climax, or (as here) the crowning point of the reasoning—the application: see on Apol. 26 D.

27. **δικαίων καὶ ἀδίκων**: Cron draws attention to the chiastic arrangement:

δικαίων ╳ αἰσχρῶν ╳ ἀγαθῶν
ἀδίκων ╳ καλῶν ╳ κακῶν　(Dyer).

47 D 31. **μᾶλλον ἢ ξύμπαντας τοὺς ἄλλους**: supra 47 B μᾶλλον ἢ ᾗ ξύμπασι τοῖς ἄλλοις.

32. **εἰ μὴ ἀκολουθήσομεν, διαφθεροῦμεν ἐκεῖνο καὶ λωβησόμεθα.** εἰ μή with fut. ind. is more vivid and impassioned than ἢν μή with aor. conj. λωβᾶσθαι is to add insult to injury. ἐκεῖνο is νοῦς: cf. Rep. VII. 527 D—E ἐν τούτοις τοῖς μαθήμασιν ἑκάστου ὄργανόν τι ψυχῆς ἐκκαθαίρεταί τε καὶ ἀναζωπυρεῖται ἀπολλύμενον καὶ τυφλούμενον ὑπὸ τῶν ἄλλων ἐπιτηδευμάτων, κρεῖτ-

τον δν σωθῆναι μυρίων ὀμμάτων· μόνῳ γὰρ αὐτῷ ἀλήθεια ὁρᾶται
(and truth is seen by νοῦς, cf. Rep. VI. 508 C—D and Symp.
212 A). Observe that the doctrine of the duality of soul and
body is implied throughout the whole of this passage: it is one of
the most distinctive traits of Plato's teaching, as it was of his master's:
see Phaed. 79 C, 82 E (the soul investigates things by looking out of
the prison-house of the body). To Plato the body is but the ὄργανον
of the soul: Theaet. 184 D δεινὸν γάρ που, ὦ παῖ, εἰ πολλαί τινες ἐν
ἡμῖν, ὥσπερ ἐν δουρείοις ἵπποις, αἰσθήσεις ἐγκάθηνται, ἀλλὰ μὴ εἰς
μίαν τινὰ ἰδέαν, εἴτε ψυχὴν εἴτε ὅ τι δεῖ καλεῖν, πάντα ταῦτα ξυντείνει,
ᾗ διὰ τούτων οἷον ὀργάνων αἰσθανόμεθα ὅσα αἰσθητά: compare also
Rep. V. 469 E, where those who wreak their vengeance on the dead
bodies of their enemies are likened to hounds αἳ τοῖς λίθοις οἷς ἂν
βληθῶσι χαλεπαίνουσι τοῦ βαλόντος οὐχ ἁπτόμεναι.

33. δ—ἀπώλλυτο: 'which, we used to say, is improved by
right, and disabled by wrong' (Church): see last note. For this
use of the imperfect cf. Rep. VI. 490 A ἡγεῖτο δ' αὐτῷ, εἰ νῷ ἔχεις,
πρῶτον μὲν ἀλήθεια κτλ. Goodwin MT. 8. The use of ἦν='is
ex hypothesi' does not differ greatly from this.

CHAPTER VIII.

Here Socrates finally disposes of the first point raised by Crito,
viz. that we should regard the opinions of the many, and proceeds
to discuss the second (see above, 44 D)—that the many can take away
our lives.

2. ὑπὸ τοῦ νοσώδους. νοσῶδες is not here='diseased', but
'causing disease', 'unwholesome',)(ὑγιεινόν: so in Theaet. 171 E
τὰ ὑγιεινὰ καὶ νοσώδη.

3. πειθόμενοι μὴ τῇ τῶν ἐπαϊόντων δόξῃ. Note the position
of μή: Plato has arranged his words so as to express the double
meaning of μὴ πειθόμενοι τῇ τῶν ἐπαϊόντων δόξῃ, and πειθόμενοι τῇ
τῶν μὴ κτλ., for the text at once suggests ἀλλὰ τῇ τῶν μὴ ἐπαϊόντων.
Compare Legg. II. 671 D νήφοντας τῶν μὴ νηφόντων στρατηγούς,
ὧν δὴ χωρὶς μέθη διαμάχεσθαι δεινότερον ἢ πολεμίοις εἶναι μὴ μετὰ
ἀρχόντων ἀθορύβων sc. ἀλλὰ μετὰ ἀρχόντων νηφόντων. Hirschig
foolishly corrupts the text to πειθόμενοι τῇ τῶν μὴ ἐπαϊόντων δόξῃ.

6. τοῦτο τὸ σῶμα. τοῦτο is of course in the predicate: Wohlrab is wrong in reading τοῦτο σῶμα with Buttmann; for σῶμα without

the article is 'body' generally, i.e. 'matter', not '*the* body': cf.
Symp. 211 A οὐδ᾽ αὖ φαντασθήσεται αὐτῷ τὸ καλὸν οἷον πρόσωπόν
τι οὐδὲ χεῖρες οὐδὲ ἄλλο οὐδὲν ὧν σῶμα (i.e. body, matter) μετέχει.

8. μετὰ μοχθηροῦ. The preposition μετά is far more frequent
than σύν in Plato, as in Attic Greek generally (except Xenophon):
σύν denotes a much closer connection. μοχθηρός like πονηρός meant
originally 'afflicted' (as here), then 'depraved', 'corrupt', for τοῖος
γὰρ νόος ἐστὶν ἐπιχθονίων ἀνθρώπων οἷον ἐπ᾽ ἦμαρ ἄγῃσι πατὴρ
ἀνδρῶν τε θεῶν τε (Hom. Od. XVIII. 136—137). So also Ar. Av.
493 χλαῖναν γὰρ ἀπώλεσ᾽ ὁ μοχθηρὸς Φρυγίων ἐρίων διὰ τοῦτον:
compare (for πονηρός) Solon Frag. 14 οὐδὲ μάκαρς οὐδεὶς πέλεται βροτός,
ἀλλὰ πονηροὶ πάντες, and Hesiod Frag. 95. 1 (ed. Göttling) πονη-
ρότατον καὶ ἄριστον (of Heracles). It is we and not the Greeks
who by suffering are made strong. Cf. Simonides Frag. 5. 10—13
ed. Bergk.

10. οὐδαμῶς. Plato held that it is better to die than to suffer
incurable disease: Gorg. 512 A—a passage which is parallel to this
both in respect of the illustration and the application—εἰ μέν τις
μεγάλοις καὶ ἀνιάτοις νοσήμασι κατὰ τὸ σῶμα συνεχόμενος μὴ ἀπεπνίγη,
οὗτος μὲν ἄθλιός ἐστιν ὅτι οὐκ ἀπέθανε κτλ.: where see Thompson on
the "meditative skipper". The whole subject is discussed in Rep.
III. 405 foll. The presence of too many doctors, says Plato, proves
that a city is physically unsound just as a plethora of δικασταί proves
that it is unsound morally: ibid. 410 A it is prescribed that doctors
in the ideal state shall only endeavour to cure τοὺς μὲν εὐφυεῖς τὰ
σώματα καὶ τὰς ψυχάς—τοὺς δὲ μή, ὅσοι μὲν κατὰ σῶμα τοιοῦτοι,
ἀποθνήσκειν ἐάσουσι, τοὺς δὲ κατὰ τὴν ψυχὴν κακοφυεῖς καὶ
ἀνιάτους αὐτοὶ ἀποκτενοῦσιν. This is declared to be the most
merciful way of treating the patients themselves and the best thing
for the State. Herodicus is censured as μακρὸν—τὸν θάνατον αὐτῷ
ποιήσας (406 B), because he prolonged his life by a course of
medical treatment: the right view is that οὐδενὶ σχολὴ διὰ βίου
κάμνειν ἰατρευομένῳ (ib. 406 C).

11. ἀλλὰ μετ᾽ ἐκείνου ἆρ᾽ ἡμῖν κτλ. So I read with the Bodleian: the editors mostly follow less good MSS and read ἀλλ᾽—ἆρα.
The ἀλλά introduces a fresh point in the argument: cf. Apol. 37 C
ἀλλὰ χρημάτων, καὶ δεδέσθαι ἕως ἂν ἐκτίσω; For the collocation
ἀλλ᾽ ἆρα (ἆρα in this connection generally invites the answer 'no')
compare Lysis 208 D ἀλλ᾽ ἆρα ἐπειδὰν οἴκαδε ἔλθῃς παρὰ τὴν μητέρα,
ἐκείνη σε ἐᾷ ποιεῖν ὅ τι ἂν βούλῃ κτλ.; Euthyd. 292 C ἀλλ᾽ ἆρα

πάντας καὶ πάντα ἀγαθούς;—οὐκ οἶμαι ἔγωγε, ὦ Σώκρατες. Here
ἄρα is separated from ἀλλά in order to let the full stress of the
sentence-accent fall on μετ' ἐκείνου, which introduces the application.

12. ᾧ τὸ ἄδικον μὲν λωβᾶται. Elsewhere Plato uses the accusative after λωβᾶσθαι: the dative is here preferred in order to
avoid the appearance of ambiguity. Ar. Eq. 1408 ἵν' ἴδωσιν αὐτὸν
οἷς ἐλωβᾶθ' οἱ ξένοι. The verb of kindred meaning λυμαίνεσθαι—
not found in Plato—may also be construed with a dative as well as
with an accusative.

13. ἢ φαυλότερον ἡγούμεθα κτλ. Compare Xen. Mem. IV. 3.
14 ἀλλὰ μὴν καὶ ἀνθρώπου γε ψυχὴ ἢ εἴπερ τι καὶ ἄλλο τῶν ἀνθρωπίνων
τοῦ θείου μετέχει κτλ. and Prot. 313 A ὃ δὲ περὶ πλείονος τοῦ
σώματος ἡγεῖ, τὴν ψυχήν, καὶ ἐν ᾧ πάντ' ἐστὶ τὰ σὰ ἢ εὖ ἢ κακῶς
πράττειν, χρηστοῦ ἢ πονηροῦ γενομένου κτλ. Socrates never wearied
of asserting the dignity of the soul.

14. περὶ ὃ ἥ τε ἀδικία κτλ. In Rep. X. 609 B injustice is de- 48 A
scribed as a disease of the soul: τί οὖν; ἦν δ' ἐγώ· ψυχῇ ἄρα οὐκ
ἔστιν ὃ ποιεῖ αὐτὴν κακήν; καὶ μάλα, ἔφη, ἃ νῦν δὴ διῇμεν πάντα,
ἀδικία τε καὶ ἀκολασία καὶ δειλία καὶ ἀμαθία.

19. οὐκ ἄρα—πάνυ ἡμῖν οὕτω: οὕτω goes with πάνυ. I think
this more probable than to take οὐ πάνυ together: πάνυ seems too
emphatic to admit of this interpretation.

20. ἀλλ' ὅ τι ὁ ἐπαΐων. The Bodleian has ὅτι, which may be
right, as the Greeks probably considered ὅ τι and ὅτι to be the
same word (=quod): see my Apology p. 123.

22. πρῶτον μέν instead of being followed by εἶτα or ἔπειτα (δέ)
corresponds to ἀλλὰ μὲν δή in line 25 below: the second argument
of Crito is quoted as an objection to Socrates' refutation of the first:
see on πρῶτον μέν in 46 C.

εἰσηγεῖ, εἰσηγούμενος. The word εἰσηγεῖσθαι (auctor esse)
means to introduce a subject or a proposal in a formal way: see
Thuc. IV. 76. 2 Πτοιοδώρου—ἐσηγουμένου τάδε αὐτοῖς παρεσκευά-
σθη, and Pl. Symp. 176 E τὸ μετὰ τοῦτο εἰσηγοῦμαι τὴν μὲν ἄρτι
εἰσελθοῦσαν αὐλητρίδα χαίρειν ἐᾶν κτλ. Perhaps Plato chooses the
word in order to suggest that Crito as it were εἰσῆγε δίκην κατὰ τῶν
νόμων—the Laws being on their defence: see Introd. pp. vii—xi.

25. ἀλλὰ μὲν δή: here begins Socrates' reply to the second
point raised by Crito: see above 44 D. μὲν δή='for that matter',
'as to that': cf. Gorg. 471 A εἴπερ γε, ὦ φίλε, ἄδικος. ἀλλὰ μὲν δὴ
πῶς οὐκ ἄδικος; 492 E ἀλλὰ μὲν δὴ καὶ ὥς γε σὺ λέγεις δεινὸς ὁ βίος:

Rep. III. 406 A καὶ μὲν δὴ—ἀτοπόν γε τὸ πῶμα οὕτως ἔχοντι: ibid. III. 409 B.

26. ἀποκτιννύναι is preferred by Plato to ἀποκτείνειν.

48 B   27. δῆλα δὴ καὶ ταῦτα κτλ. = 'of course, that is also evident: yes, Socrates, he will say so'. If the text is right, I think δῆλα δὴ καὶ ταῦτα is an aside: the answer to Socrates' remark is contained in φαίη γὰρ ἄν. Crito (who is not yet convinced by Socrates' reasoning) first declares that the power of the many to put one to death (ταῦτα) is as obvious as the necessity of regarding what they think of one (καὶ): he then assents to Socrates' remark. See above 44 D αὐτὰ δὲ δῆλα τὰ παρόντα νυνί, ὅτι οἷοί τ' εἰσὶν οἱ πολλοί κτλ.

With Cron and Kral I have retained the vulgate, because I think it presents the fewest difficulties. Wohlrab gives δῆλα δὴ καὶ ταῦτα to Socrates, φαίη γὰρ ἄν, ὦ Σώκρατες to Crito, and ἀληθῆ λέγεις to Socrates: Schanz brackets φαίη γὰρ ἄν, and gives both δῆλα δὴ καὶ ταῦτα and ἀληθῆ λέγεις to Crito: Göbel prints " δῆλα δὴ καὶ ταῦτα", φαίη γὰρ ἂν ὦ Σώκρατες. Σω. ἀληθῆ λέγεις. I think the text is probably right as it stands: but if not, I should transpose and read φαίη γὰρ ἂν δῆλα δὴ καὶ ταῦτα, ὦ Σώκρατες, taking δῆλα δὴ as an adverb as it is in the MSS (δηλαδή).

29. ὦ θαυμάσιε: see on ὦ δαιμόνιε Σώκρατες in 44 B.

οὗτός τε: τε corresponds to καὶ in καὶ τόνδε αὖ σκόπει line 31. There is virtually an anacoluthon, since οὗτός τε ὁ λόγος—δοκεῖ leads us to expect καὶ ὅδε αὖ ὁ λόγος (sc. δοκεῖ ἔτι ὅμοιος εἶναι), ὅτι οὐ τὸ ζῆν κτλ.: but whether the second principle is still binding or not, has not yet been decided: whence καὶ τόνδε αὖ σκόπει κτλ.

30. ὅμοιος εἶναι καὶ πρότερον: the MSS read τῷ καὶ πρότερον: but as τῷ πρότερον for τῷ προτέρῳ or τῷ πρότερον εἰρημένῳ is, to say the least of it, unusual, and the καὶ is awkward, I follow Wex, Madvig and recent editors (except Göbel) in reading καὶ πρότερον. ὅμοιος καὶ πρότερον = similis quam antea: see above 46 B σχεδόν τι ὅμοιοι φαίνονταί μοι καὶ τοὺς αὐτοὺς πρεσβεύω καὶ τιμῶ, οὕσπερ καὶ πρότερον.

32. οὐ τὸ ζῆν περὶ πλείστου ποιητέον, ἀλλὰ τὸ εὖ ζῆν. Socrates held this view during the trial: see Apol. 28 B and ch. XXIII. Compare Gorg. 512 E μὴ γὰρ τοῦτο μέν, τὸ ζῆν ὁπόσον δὴ χρόνον, τόν γε ὡς ἀληθῶς ἄνδρα ἐατέον ἐστὶ καὶ οὐ φιλοψυχητέον, ἀλλὰ—σκεπτέον τίν' ἂν τρόπον τοῦτον ὃν μέλλει χρόνον βιῶναι ὡς ἄριστα βιώῃ.

35. τὸ δὲ εὖ—ταὐτόν ἐστιν: Cron remarks that this clause is

necessary because εὖ ζῆν has a double meaning (see above on 47 B
τῷ ἐπιστάτῃ καὶ ἐπαΐοντι): it is necessary also to identify εὖ with
δικαίως because the next chapter opens with the question πότερον
δίκαιον ἐμὲ ἐνθένδε πειρᾶσθαι ἐξιέναι.

It should be noted that ταὐτόν τοσοῦτον τοιοῦτον τηλικοῦτον are
regular in Plato, not ταὐτό and the like: see on Apol. 24 C. Schanz
now thinks it probable that Plato always used the forms in -ν: see
his Preface to the Laws p. vi.

CHAPTER IX.

This and the following chapter make a kind of interlude. Socrates
has now reached his principle or λόγος, viz. ὅτι οὐ τὸ ζῆν περὶ
πλείστου ποιητέον, ἀλλὰ τὸ δικαίως ζῆν. Before introducing the
Laws to prove that if Socrates made his escape he would violate this
principle, Socrates pauses to emphasize the full force and meaning
of this λόγος, and the irrelevancy of every other. Throughout this
and the following chapters it must be borne in mind that Socrates
identified τὸ δίκαιον with τὸ νόμιμον: see Introd. p. xiii.

1. **ἐκ τῶν ὁμολογουμένων**: the present as in ὅπερ λέγω and the
like (Graser quoted by Wohlrab). See above on ὅπερ λέγω in 45 B.
τοῦτο refers forward to πότερον δίκαιον κτλ.

2. **πότερον δίκαιον κτλ.** δίκαιον is 'right': see on 45 C above.
Crito had put the question on the same grounds in the passage referred to ἔτι δέ—οὐδὲ δίκαιόν μοι δοκεῖς ἐπιχειρεῖν πρᾶγμα. ἀφιέναι
is not 'to permit' (ἐφιέναι), but 'to let go free', as in Apol. 29 C
ἀφίεμέν σε.

4. **ἢ οὐ δίκαιον**: more emphatic and clear than ἢ οὔ: so in B 48 C
above μένει ἢ οὐ μένει.

6. **ἃς δὲ σὺ λέγεις τὰς σκέψεις**: viz. in 45 A—46 A. The relative
clause is placed first so as to let emphasis be thrown on σὺ)(ἐγώ:
αἱ δὲ σκέψεις ἃς σὺ λέγεις would be much less pointed. Cron remarks
that when the antecedent is adopted into the relative clause, the
article is more usually omitted, as in οὓς ἡ πόλις νομίζει θεοὺς οὐ
νομίζων. Tr. 'as for the considerations you mention, about' etc.

8. **ὡς ἀληθῶς**: see on 46 D above.

9. **σκέμματα ᾖ.** σκέμματα is of course in the predicate. The
antecedent to ταῦτα is not σκέψεις but ἀναλώσεως χρημάτων καὶ δόξης

καὶ παίδων τροφῆς.   On μὴ ᾖ (= nescio an sit) see Goodwin MT. 83:
probably some word expressing fear or apprehension ought to be
understood: see on Apol. 39 Α μὴ οὐ τοῦτ' ᾖ χαλεπόν.

τῶν ῥᾳδίως ἀποκτιννύντων κτλ.   Gorg. 521 C (quoted above on
44 D) ἀνόητος ἄρα εἰμί, ὦ Καλλίκλεις, ὡς ἀληθῶς, εἰ μὴ οἴομαι ἐν τῇδε
τῇ πόλει ὀντινοῦν ἂν ὅ τι τύχοι τοῦτο παθεῖν.   We are of course
not justified in seeing here an allusion to the alleged remorse of the
Athenians after Socrates' death: the tradition about their repentance
is late and untrustworthy: see Grote, Vol. VIII. p. 302.   For ἄν
with the participle in apodosis cf. Legg. VI. 781 Α πολὺ ἄμεινον ἂν
ἔχοντα, εἰ νόμων ἔτυχεν: Goodwin MT. 114.   The word ἀναβιώ-
σκεσθαι more often means 'to come to life again': for the causative
sense cf. Phaed. 89 Β ἐάνπερ γε—μὴ δυνώμεθα αὐτὸν ἀναβιώσα-
σθαι.

10.   οὐδενὶ ξὺν νῷ.   Wohlrab compares Ar. Nub. 580 ἢν γὰρ ᾖ
τις ἔξοδος μηδενὶ ξὺν νῷ.   Plato occasionally uses ξύν in such adverbial phrases, e.g. ξὺν πολλῷ θορύβῳ Rep. VI. 492 Β: otherwise it
generally occurs in religious uses like Legg. III. 682 Α ξύν τισι Χάρισι
καὶ Μούσαις, or where the connection is a very close one, as in Legg.
III. 678 C ξὺν ταῖς τέχναις ὡς ἔπος εἰπεῖν πάντα σχεδὸν ἀπολώλει; Gorg.
513 Α ξὺν τοῖς φιλτάτοις ἡ αἵρεσις ἡμῖν ἔσται ταύτης τῆς δυνάμεως τῆς
ἐν τῇ πόλει: see also note on μετά in 47 E.

τούτων τῶν πολλῶν: οὗτος like the Latin iste expresses contempt.
Note in the next sentence the emphatic place assigned to ἡμῖν)(τοῖς
πολλοῖς.

11.   ὁ λόγος οὕτως αἱρεῖ = 'ratio ita evincit' (Cron) is a frequent
phrase in Plato: see Parm. 141 D ὥς γε ὁ λόγος αἱρεῖ.   Sometimes
the object is expressed as in Rep. X. 607 Β ὁ γὰρ λόγος ἡμᾶς ᾕρει.
Near akin is the use of αἱρεῖν = 'to secure a conviction', as in Apol.
28 Α τοῦτ' ἔστιν ὃ ἐμὲ αἱρήσει, ἐάνπερ αἱρῇ, where see note.

12.   νῦν δή.   See on 46 D above.

48 D   14.   καὶ χάριτας: the plural is preferred to the singular, not
only because Socrates is speaking for Crito as well as for himself,
but because it balances the plural χρήματα more neatly.   It is hardly
necessary to supply εἰδότες from τελοῦντες: τελεῖν χάριν (χάριτας) is
to 'pay a debt of gratitude'.

15.   ἐξάγοντές τε καὶ ἐξαγόμενοι: ἐξάγων τε καὶ ἐξαγόμενος would
be more logical and less grammatical.

τῇ ἀληθείᾳ: see on ὡς ἀληθῶς 46 D.

17.   μὴ οὐ δέῃ ὑπολογίζεσθαι: for the syntax compare note on

μὴ ὡς ἀληθῶς—ῇ in 48 C. ὑπολογίζεσθαι is 'to entertain a reflection pointing to the opposite line of conduct from that which we are, or ought to be, pursuing': see on Apol. 28 B. We have the same sentiment and the same mode of expression in Apol. 28 D δεῖ—μένοντα κινδυνεύειν, μηδὲν ὑπολογιζόμενον μήτε θάνατον μήτε ἄλλο μηδὲν πρὸ τοῦ αἰσχροῦ. παραμένοντας differs from μένοντας as 'staying here' from 'standing fast' or 'holding our ground'.

19. **οὔτε ἄλλο ὁτιοῦν πάσχειν πρὸ τοῦ ἀδικεῖν:** so the MSS. Schanz reads οὔτ' εἰ after Forster. εἰ δεῖ is to be supplied from the preceding clause.

20. **καλῶς—λέγειν—ὅρα δὲ τί δρῶμεν:** it is time for deeds, not words: supra 46 A ἀλλὰ βουλεύου, μᾶλλον δὲ οὐδὲ βουλεύεσθαι ἔτι ὥρα, ἀλλὰ βεβουλεῦσθαι. δρῶμεν is the deliberative conjunctive.

24. **παῦσαι.** In Attic 'stop!' is παῦσαι or παῦε (not παῦου, 48 E though in Homer παύεο is found). παῦε is the only form of this word used intransitively in good writers: the plural is παύεσθε and παύσασθε: see Cobet V. L. pp. 264, 367, and Rutherford on Babrius 28. 8.

26. **πεῖσαί σε, ἀλλὰ μὴ ἄκοντος ταῦτα πράττειν.** The MS reading πεῖσαί σε ταῦτα πράττειν, ἀλλὰ μὴ ἄκοντος cannot be right: for apart from the awkwardness of ἀλλὰ μὴ ἄκοντος, ταῦτα πράττειν could only mean 'to let me remain and die': an impossible meaning, since it leaves ταῦτα without an antecedent, Socrates as yet professing not to have made up his mind but to be willing to follow ὅπῃ ἂν ὁ λόγος ἄγῃ: see line 22 σκοπῶμεν, ὦ ἀγαθέ, κοινῇ κτλ. I follow Meiser (Fleckeisen's Jahrb. 1874, p. 40) in transposing ταῦτα πράττειν and ἀλλὰ μὴ ἄκοντος (sc. σοῦ): ταῦτα πράττειν (= 'to do what I do', 'to act herein') depends on περὶ πολλοῦ ποιοῦμαι, and is coordinate with and not subordinate to πεῖσαι, which is used absolutely. Translate: 'for I think it important to persuade you, and not to act in this without your consent'. Cron, Schanz and Kral retain the MS order, changing πεῖσαι to πείσας, with Buttmann, Hermann and Madvig: Wohlrab alone among recent editors retains the MS reading. By Wex (Fleckeisen's Jahrb. for 1856, p. 669) πεῖσαι is rejected as "ein erklärendes Glossem zu dem falsch verstandenem πράττειν. Platon also schrieb ὡς ἐγώ—ποιοῦμαί σε ταῦτα πράττειν, ἀλλὰ μὴ ἄκοντος sc. πρᾶττε". Göbel discusses the passage at length in his Fulda program 1882 p. 10 foll., and claims to have solved all difficulties by the change of πεῖσαι to παῦσαι: but in reality this is

only mending one fault by two others, for (a) παῦσαι would inevitably
lead to ἄκοντα: (b) ἀλλὰ μή is not 'aber nicht', but 'nicht'; i.e. it
must introduce not a mere qualification, but a direct antithesis to
some word in the preceding clause: and πεῖσαι (or πείσας) is exactly
such a word. The choice clearly lies between Meiser's view and
that of Cron: I prefer the former, because (a) even if πείσας were
right I think Plato would either have written περὶ πολλοῦ ποιοῦμαι
πείσας σε, ἀλλὰ μὴ ἄκοντος, ταῦτα πράττειν, or (less likely) περὶ
πολλοῦ ποιοῦμαι ταῦτα πράττειν πείσας σε, ἀλλὰ μὴ ἄκοντος, and
(b) because in ταῦτα πράττειν = 'do what I am doing', 'act in this
matter', the force of ταῦτα seems to me more obscure if it follows
σε than if it follows ἄκοντος.

27. ὅρα—τὴν ἀρχὴν ἐάν κτλ. For ὅρα followed by ἐάν compare
(with Wohlrab) Rep. IV. 432 C ὅρα οὖν καὶ προθυμοῦ κατιδεῖν ἐάν
πως πρότερος ἐμοῦ ἴδῃς καὶ ἐμοὶ φράσῃς. ἐάν is not here = 'whether'
(a meaning it never bears), but 'si forte', 'in case': in such expressions there is no real ellipse of the apodosis: see Monro's Homeric
Grammar, p. 212.

τὴν ἀρχήν is 'the outset', 'the start': from its use in such
examples as the present it came to mean 'principle', as so often
in Aristotle.

49 A   29. ᾗ ἂν μάλιστα οἴη, i.e. in the way to which your opinion
most inclines: ᾗ is adverbial and goes with οἴη, as in οἴεσθαι ταύτῃ:
ἔχειν is not to be understood.

CHAPTER X.

In this chapter Crito is made to admit (a) that it is wrong to
requite wrong with wrong or evil with evil, and (b) that it is our
duty to carry out in practice that which we have in theory admitted
to be right. Introduction p. xii.

1. οὐδενὶ τρόπῳ—ἀδικητέον εἶναι. For the syntax compare
Gorg. 507 D τὸν βουλόμενον—εὐδαίμονα εἶναι σωφροσύνην μὲν
διωκτέον καὶ ἀσκητέον κτλ., and for the sentiment itself Apol.
37 B πεπεισμένος δὴ ἐγὼ μηδένα ἀδικεῖν πολλοῦ δέω ἐμαυτόν γε ἀδικήσειν: Gorg. 469 B μέγιστον τῶν κακῶν τυγχάνει ὂν τὸ ἀδικεῖν: and
Rep. I. 335 D.

2. ἢ τινὶ—τινὶ δὲ οὔ: τίς is here accented because it is em-

phatic: see on Apol. 26 C (εἶναι τινὰς θεούς), where I refer to Theaetetus 147 B τινὸς γὰρ ἐπιστήμην ἀποκρίνεται οὐ τοῦτ' ἐρωτηθείς.

3. **ἢ οὐδαμῶς τό γε ἀδικεῖν**: note the force of γε: τό γε ἀδικεῖν nearly =τὸ ἀδικεῖν ἅτε ἀδικόν ὄν: cf. infra 49 B, line 14.

4. **ὡς πολλάκις—ὡμολογήθη.** It has been doubted by Zeller and others whether the doctrine here maintained was ever held by the historical Socrates: but it seems likely that it was. In harmony with his egoistic principles, Socrates denied that it is ever right to wrong another, because wrongdoing has an injurious influence on one's own soul: see Introd. p. xii.

5. **ἢ πᾶσαι.** In the MSS ὅπερ καὶ ἄρτι ἐλέγετο is written before ἢ πᾶσαι: but as there is nothing to which the words can be referred, I agree with recent editors in omitting them. The alternative (Meiser) is to write ὅπερ καὶ ἄρτι ἐλέγετο after ἢ and take the words as an allusion to 46 D νῦν δὲ κατάδηλος ἄρα ἐγένετο, ὅτι ἄλλως [ἕνεκα λόγου] ἐλέγετο, ἦν δὲ παιδιὰ καὶ φλυαρία ὡς ἀληθῶς.

7. **ἐκκεχυμέναι.** The metaphor (as Göbel remarks) is probably from losing or throwing goods overboard at sea: cf. Rep. VIII. 553 B πταίσαντα ὥσπερ πρὸς ἕρματι τῇ πόλει καὶ ἐκχέαντα τά τε αὑτοῦ καὶ ἑαυτόν. So in Aesch. Pers. 826 μηδέ τις—ὄλβον ἐκχέῃ μέγαν: compare 46 B above τοὺς δὲ λόγους οὓς ἐν τῷ ἔμπροσθεν ἔλεγον, οὐ δύναμαι νῦν ἐκβαλεῖν.

8. **πάλαι—ἄρα.** πάλαι goes with ἐλάθομεν—διαφέροντες: ἄρα as usual expresses surprise: see on Apol. 34 C ἐγὼ δὲ οὐδὲν ἄρα τούτων ποιήσω;

τηλικοίδε. After τηλικοίδε the MSS read γέροντες ἄνδρες: I think with Cron and Schanz that γέροντες is a gloss on τηλικοίδε. Fischer and Wohlrab defend the word on the ground that γέροντες ἄνδρες makes a good antithesis to παίδων: but the phrase γέροντες ἄνδρες is a trifle awkward, and ἄνδρες alone seems to me more forcible as the opposite of παίδων.

9. **σπουδῇ** is emphatic, nearly =σπουδῇ ἀλλ' οὐ παιδιᾷ (suggested by παίδων in the next line).

10. **παίδων οὐδὲν διαφέροντες** is almost a proverbial phrase, as 49 B Wohlrab remarks: compare Theaet. 177 B ἡ ῥητορικὴ ἐκείνη πως ἀπομαραίνεται, ὥστε παίδων μηδὲν δοκεῖν διαφέρειν: Prot. 342 E ὥστε φαίνεσθαι τὸν προσδιαλεγόμενον παιδὸς μηδὲν βελτίω. Here and indeed generally διαφέρειν means 'to be better than' and not simply 'to differ'.

A. C.   6

11. **παντὸς μᾶλλον** = 'assuredly' (i.e. more than anything) is frequent in Plato, e.g. Prot. 344 B παντὸς μᾶλλον ἔλεγχός ἐστι.

12. **εἴτε φασὶν οἱ πολλοὶ εἴτε μή.** For the form of the sentence compare Apol. 27 C εἴτ᾽ οὖν καινὰ εἴτε παλαιά, ἀλλ᾽ οὖν δαιμόνιά γε νομίζω κατὰ τὸν σὸν λόγον. Asyndeton is regular in this kind of explanatory clause: see on Apol. 22 A. I have printed a colon before εἴτε φασίν, cf. Apol. l. c. ὅμως in line 14 thus becomes more easy and natural.

13. **εἴτε καί** = 'or if you like': so in Apol. 27 E ὥσπερ ἂν εἴ τις ἵππων μὲν παῖδας ἡγοῖτο ἢ καὶ ὄνων.

14. **τό γε ἀδικεῖν:** see on 49 A, line 3.

καὶ κακὸν καὶ αἰσχρόν. In Gorg. 474 C foll. it is shewn that ἀδικεῖν is both κάκιον and αἴσχιον than ἀδικεῖσθαι. Note the symmetry throughout this speech of Socrates: it begins with οὐδενὶ τρόπῳ and ends with παντὶ τρόπῳ: and the two alternatives are presented in such a way that the one which finally prevails is placed both first and last: the order is a.b.a.b.a.

19. **οὐδὲ ἀδικούμενον ἄρα ἀνταδικεῖν:** ἄρα is of course 'therefore': for ἀδικούμενον ἀνταδικεῖν is ἀδικεῖν πως. Socrates does not in this assume that he has been wronged by the *laws:* only by men: see on 54 C.

ὡς οἱ πολλοὶ οἴονται. The ordinary Greek view is well summed up in the prayer of Solon (Frag. 13. 4—5) εἶναι δὲ γλυκὺν ὧδε φίλοις, ἐχθροῖσι δὲ πικρόν, τοῖσι μὲν αἰδοῖον, τοῖσι δὲ δεινὸν ἰδεῖν. Just so Medea in Euripides (807—810) μηδείς με φαύλην κἀσθενῆ νομιζέτω μηδ᾽ ἡσυχαίαν, ἀλλὰ θατέρου τρόπου, βαρεῖαν ἐχθροῖς καὶ φίλοισιν εὐμενῆ· τῶν γὰρ τοιούτων εὐκλεέστατος βίος. Socrates himself declares that this was the prevailing morality in Greece: Mem. II. 3. 14 καὶ μὴν πλείστου γε δοκεῖ ἀνὴρ ἐπαίνου ἄξιος εἶναι, ὃς ἂν φθάνῃ τοὺς μὲν πολεμίους κακῶς ποιῶν, τοὺς δὲ φίλους εὐεργετῶν: but everything is against the supposition that this view commended itself to him, and even Pittacus, if we may trust Diogenes Laertius (I. 4. 78), had already declared against it in the memorable words φίλον μὴ λέγειν κακῶς, ἀλλὰ μηδὲ ἐχθρόν. See Introd. p. xii.

49 C   22. **τί δὲ δή;** = 'once more' introduces a new departure: with τί δέ; (infra line 24) the departure is less new: from ἀδικεῖν to κακουργεῖν the transition is greater than from κακουργεῖν to ἀντικακουργεῖν.

23. **οὐ δεῖ δήπου:** contrast this with οὐ φαίνεται in 21: here at

least Crito can answer without hesitation, for κακουργεῖν suggests
the idea of a criminal or malefactor: see L. and S. s. v.

27. **τὸ γάρ που κακῶς ποιεῖν κτλ.** In Rep. I. 335 B foll.
ἀδικεῖν is identified with κακοὺς ποιεῖν rather than κακῶς ποιεῖν
through the middle term βλάπτειν.

30. **κακῶς ποιεῖν—πάσχῃ ὑπ' αὐτῶν** is circumlocutory for ἀντικακουργεῖν. For οὐδ' ἂν ὁτιοῦν πάσχῃ=ne tum quidem si quidvis
patiatur, compare Rep. VII. 522 E εἰ καὶ ὁτιοῦν μέλλει τάξεων ἐπαΐειν:
Polit. 297 B οὐκ ἂν πλῆθος οὐδ' ὠντινωνοῦν. The subject to πάσχῃ
is understood from the unexpressed subject to ἀνταδικεῖν and κακῶς
ποιεῖν: see note on Apol. 29 A δοκεῖν γὰρ εἰδέναι ἐστὶν ἃ οὐκ οἶδεν.

32. **καθομολογῶν**: the κατά points to the gradual piecemeal
character of the admissions: cf. Gorg. 499 B πάλαι τοί σου ἀκρῶμαι
καθομολογῶν, ἐνθυμούμενος ὅτι κἂν παίζων τίς σοι ἐνδῷ ὁτιοῦν,
τούτου ἄσμενος ἔχει ὥσπερ τὰ μειράκια: see also Rep. VI. 487 B—C
where it is said that Socrates leads one on little by little till lo!
when at the end all the little admissions are added up μέγα τὸ
σφάλμα καὶ ἐναντίον τοῖς πρώτοις.

33. **οἶδα γὰρ ὅτι ὀλίγοις τισὶ—δόξει.** This confession that his 49 D
doctrines are for the few and not for the many is more in the vein of
Plato than of Socrates. It is possible that Socrates may have been
led to hold this language by his condemnation on an unjust charge:
but while actively engaged on his mission he was as far as possible
from despairing, as is clear from Xen. Mem. III. 5. See Introduction p. xv.

34. **οἷς οὖν—τούτοις οὐκ ἔστι κοινὴ βουλή.** Compare Apol.
31 E—32 A and Phaed. 82 D τούτοις μὲν ἅπασιν—ἐκεῖνοι οἷς τι μέλει
τῆς ἑαυτῶν ψυχῆς—χαίρειν εἰπόντες οὐ κατὰ ταὐτὰ πορεύονται αὐτοῖς
ὡς νοῦν εἰδόσιν ὅπῃ ἔρχονται: ibid. 64 B—C εἴπωμεν—πρὸς ἡμᾶς
αὐτούς, χαίρειν εἰπόντες ἐκείνοις (sc. τοῖς πολλοῖς).

36. **ἀλλήλων καταφρονεῖν**: the many laugh at the philosopher
(Rep. VII. 517 A), and if the philosopher laughs at them, ἧττον ἂν
καταγέλαστος ὁ γέλως αὐτῷ εἴη ἢ ὁ ἐπὶ τῇ ἄνωθεν ἐκ φωτὸς ἡκούσῃ (sc.
ψυχῇ): Rep. VII. 518 B.

38. **κοινωνεῖς** is used with reference to κοινὴ βουλή in 38: so
infra in 42. ἐντεῦθεν in the same line=ἐκ τούτου τοῦ λόγου and is
explained by ὡς οὐδέποτε κτλ.: compare (with Jacobs) Prot.
324 A ἔνθα δὴ πᾶς παντὶ θυμοῦται καὶ νουθετεῖ, δῆλον ὅτι ὡς ἐξ
ἐπιμελείας καὶ μαθήσεως κτητῆς οὔσης.

40. **οὔτε τοῦ ἀνταδικεῖν.** After these words we might expect

οὔτε τοῦ κακουργεῖν, but as Göbel points out ἀδικεῖν has already been identified with κακουργεῖν (in c above, line 27): and besides it is on the injustice of τὸ ἀντικακουργεῖν rather than of τὸ κακουργεῖν that the rest of the dialogue turns.

49 E   42. τῆς ἀρχῆς: said with reference to ἀρχώμεθα in 28: see note on 48 E above.

44. τὸ μετὰ τοῦτο='my next point': see on Apol. 39 B.

48. μᾶλλον δ' ἐρωτῶ=vel potius interrogo: Socrates said his say by questions oftener than by answers: see Apol. 33 B. For μᾶλλον δέ see above on 46 A.

50. ἐξαπατητέον: to believe a theory and yet not carry it into practice is a living lie: to Socrates this seemed not only wrong, but impossible, since knowledge is virtue and οὐδεὶς ἑκὼν ἁμαρτάνει: see Introd. to Apol. p. xi.

CHAPTER XI.

With this chapter the third division of the dialogue begins. Crito has now admitted the major premise which is to determine the action of Socrates, viz. that under no circumstances is it right to do wrong or requite wrong with wrong or evil with evil. The minor premise is still wanting, and to establish this Socrates introduces the Laws of Athens, who endeavour to prove that if he complied with Crito's invitation, Socrates would be guilty of wrong-doing, and retaliation in wrong-doing. In this chapter they urge that escape would be wrong because it would mean the entire negation of the State and civic life. See Introduction pp. x—xiv.

1. ἐκ τούτων='in the light of this', 'starting from these premises': so in 48 B ἐκ τῶν ὁμολογουμένων.

50 A   4. οἷς ὡμολογήσαμεν δικαίοις οὖσιν=τούτοις ἃ ὡμολογήσαμεν δίκαια ὄντα with a reference to 49 E πότερον ἃ ἄν τις ὁμολογήσῃ τῳ δίκαια ὄντα ποιητέον ἢ ἐξαπατητέον ; δίκαια ὄντα is attracted to οἷς=τούτοις ἅ: for a similar case see Apol. 37 B ἀντὶ τούτου δὴ ἕλωμαι (MSS ἕλωμαι) ὧν εὖ οἶδ' ὅτι κακῶν ὄντων i.e. τούτων ἃ εὖ οἶδ' ὅτι κακὰ ὄντα.

6. οὐκ ἔχω—οὐ γὰρ ἐννοῶ: the words are full of pathos: Crito sees but too clearly what the conclusion will be.

8. ἀλλ' ὧδε σκόπει: ᾧδε and not ὧδε is the reading of B. It is characteristic of Socrates to let the Laws speak for themselves:

like Plato he was nothing if not clear and emphatic. For a similar
example see Theaet. 166 A foll. I think too that Plato wished to
save Socrates from the charge of selfishness and lack of feeling,
when his friends were so deeply moved, and hence the fatal
argument comes not from his mouth but from the Laws.

μέλλουσιν ἡμῖν: the dative depends on ἐπιστάντες: Cron compares Symp. 192 D εἰ αὐτοῖς—ἐπιστὰς ὁ Ἥφαιστος—ἔροιτο.

9. εἴθ' ὅπως δεῖ ὀνομάσαι τοῦτο. ἀποδιδράσκειν suggests a
runaway slave or a deserter, and these words are added to spare
Crito's feelings, "mitigandae orationis causa" (Stallbaum). For
the Greek Stallbaum compares Legg. I. 633 A περὶ τῶν τῆς ἄλλης
ἀρετῆς εἴτε μερῶν εἴτε ἅττ' αὐτὰ καλεῖν χρεών ἐστι.

10. ἐλθόντες—ἔροιντο: cf. Rep. VII. 538 D ὅταν—ἐλθὸν ἐρώ-
τημα ἔρηται, τί ἐστι τὸ καλόν. The synonym τὸ κοινὸν τῆς πόλεως
is added with a view to τὴν πόλιν (line 15) and ἡ πόλις (22) afterwards. The editors refer to Prot. 319 D τὸ κοινὸν τῆς πόλεως
οὕτως ἔχει and Cic. Verr. II. 2. 114 a communi Siciliae. It is
possible that Cicero had the whole passage in view when he wrote
(Cat. I. 17) Quae (sc. patria) tecum Catilina sic agit et quodam
modo tacita loquitur.

11. ἐπιστάντες is regularly used of a vision 'standing over'
one: see Symp. 192 D (quoted on line 8 above). The word occurs
naturally to Socrates, who had a devout belief in visions: see on
ἦν δὲ δὴ τί τὸ ἐνύπνιον in 44 A. Lucr. III. 959 et necopinanti mors
ad caput adstitit.

12. ἄλλο τι ἤ=aliudne quid quam? i.e. nonne? see on Apol.
24 C: ἄλλο τι alone can bear the same meaning. With ᾧ ἐπιχειρεῖς
contrast 45 C ἐπιχειρεῖν πρᾶγμα: the influence of the preceding
ἔργῳ causes ᾧ to be preferred to the more usual ὅ.

13. τούς τε νόμους ἡμᾶς ἀπολέσαι: ἡμᾶς is emphatic, almost 50 B
deictic: the voice should pause before and after it. The laws and
constitution of Athens are arraigned before Socrates: whence ἀπολέσαι 'to kill', 'destroy', viz. by giving an adverse verdict. So
in Legg. IX. 857 A, where the metaphor is still kept up: προδότῃ
καὶ ἱεροσύλῳ καὶ τῷ τοὺς τῆς πόλεως νόμους βίᾳ ἀπολλύντι—
the parricide, as it were, of his country's laws. See Introduction
pp. vii—viii.

τὸ σὸν μέρος: 'as far as lies with you': so in 45 D above. In
ἢ δοκεῖ σοι οἷόν τε it is better to regard δοκεῖ σοι as parenthetical
('think you') and understand ἐστίν with οἷόν τε than to understand

εἶναι after δοκεῖ: cf. Phaed. 108 D ὁ βίος μοι δοκεῖ—οὐκ ἐξαρκεῖ :
see on 43 D above.

14. ἐκείνην τὴν πόλιν εἶναι: Buttmann reads πόλιν πόλιν εἶναι:
but εἶναι here= 'exist')(ἀνατετράφθαι : it is not the copula.

16. δίκαι is here 'judgments', 'decisions' not 'lawsuits': this
use is frequent in Homer, but rare in Attic. γενόμεναι=δικα-
σθεῖσαι as in line 20.

17. ἄκυροι is opposed to κύριαι: see line 21.

19. ἄλλως τε καὶ ῥήτωρ: the imagery of a trial is still kept
up: see Introduction p. vii.

20. ἀπολλυμένου: see note on line 13 above. Cron remarks
that throughout all this passage there is an allusion to the custom
of appointing συνήγοροι or advocates to defend any law which it
was proposed to repeal.

21. ὅτι introduces the direct quotation as in Apol. 21 C
ἀποφανῶν τῷ χρησμῷ ὅτι οὑτοσὶ ἐμοῦ σοφώτερός ἐστι, σὺ δ᾽ ἐμὲ
ἔφησθα: infr. 50 C.

50 C   22. ἠδίκει γάρ: the force of γάρ is clear ('Yes, I do mean to
wrong the laws) for' etc. Instead of ἠδίκει Heindorf requires
ἀδικεῖ: the present of this verb is frequently used of an injury
committed in the past because the injury is supposed to continue
till it is atoned for. But Socrates speaks as one who has outlived
the sense of injury: the imperfect ἠδίκει is thus in keeping with the
spirit of his motto ἐν εὐφημίᾳ χρὴ τελευτᾶν (Phaed. 117 E).

23. ἔκρινεν: the Aorist, not the imperfect, in spite of ἠδίκει.

CHAPTER XII.

The Laws proceed to argue that Socrates is their child and
slave, bound to render them all the obedience due to parents and
masters, or rather more, because one's fatherland should be more
to one than parents.

2. καὶ ταῦτα= 'this too', viz. the reservation that you were to
question our decrees, and disobey them if they seemed to you wrong.
The antecedent to ταῦτα is implied in the words ἠδίκει γάρ—ἔκρινεν
(50 C). The suggestion of Keck to read ταῦτά for ταῦτα obscures the
connection and leaves καί unexplained: the meaning of καί is fixed
by the following line: ἢ ἐμμένειν—δικάζῃ, i.e. 'or to abide by the

decisions delivered by the State', sc. without *any* clause of reservation.

3. **ταῖς δίκαις**: δίκαι = 'decisions', 'judgments', as in 50 B,
line 16.

4. **αὐτῶν θαυμάζοιμεν λεγόντων** = 'should be surprised at their
language': θαυμάζειν is regularly followed by a genitive of the
person: Goodwin, Gk. Gr. 222.

5. **ὅτι**: see on 50 B. Infra in line 7 καί = 'also'.

8. **τῷ ἐρωτᾶν τε καὶ ἀποκρίνεσθαι** = τῷ διαλέγεσθαι by a common
periphrasis: Stallbaum refers to Phaed. 75 D καὶ ἐν ταῖς ἐρωτήσεσιν
ἐρωτῶντες καὶ ἐν ταῖς ἀποκρίσεσιν ἀποκρινόμενοι.

10. **ἀπολλύναι**: see on 50 B, line 13. πρῶτον μέν corresponds 50 D
to ἀλλά in line 14: the second question thus becomes more vivid:
for a similar case compare 48 A and 53 B. ἐγεννήσαμεν = γενέσθαι
ἐποιήσαμεν 'called into existence': Aristotle has γεννώντων αὐτόν
(sc. τὸν οὐρανὸν) = γενέσθαι αὐτὸν λεγόντων (De Cael. II. 283ᵇ
31). The idiom is extremely common in Plato.

11. **καὶ δι' ἡμῶν ἐλάμβανεν—ἐφύτευσέν σε**; This explains
ἐγεννήσαμεν. Note λαμβάνω in the sense of 'I take to wife': so
Eur. Alc. 325 γυναῖκ' ἀρίστην ἐστὶ κομπάσαι λαβεῖν. Göbel
remarks that the imperfect calls up the circumstances and provisions
of the courtship (if there was any) and wedding: for the collocation
of the imperfect and the aorist cf. infra 52 C οὕτω σφόδρα ἡμᾶς ᾑροῦ
καὶ ὡμολόγεις—καὶ παῖδας ἐν αὐτῇ ἐποιήσω.

12. **τούτοις ἡμῶν τοῖς νόμοις**: here and in line 17 Schanz
follows Hirschig in bracketing τοῖς νόμοις (νόμοι): but the addition
of these words makes the Greek far more explicit and emphatic.
τούτοις is deictic.

13. **τοῖς περὶ τοὺς γάμους**: Cron remarks that Socrates is
thinking chiefly of the laws which established the legal validity of
marriage and as a consequence the legitimacy of the children. Some
account of the laws relating to marriage is given in Becker's Charicles
E. T. pp. 473—498.

14. **ἔχουσιν** is probably the participle : τι points to this (Cron).
For ἀλλά v. note on line 10 above.

15. **τροφήν τε καὶ παιδείαν**. Plato frequently uses this expression to denote the upbringing and education of a child: e.g.
Rep. IV. 445 E τροφῇ τε καὶ παιδείᾳ χρησάμενος ᾗ διήλθομεν.
τροφή is the wider term, including the general care of the body: in
παιδεία the care of the soul is the prominent idea.

16. **ἢ οὐ καλῶς**: ἢ—the less authenticated reading—would = Lat. An? ἢ οὐ is simply Nonne?

οἱ ἐπὶ τούτοις τεταγμένοι νόμοι: the antecedent to τούτοις is implied in τροφήν τε καὶ παιδείαν (line 14). The word παραγγέλλοντες is not to be pressed: it is doubtful to what extent Athenian parents were compelled by law to educate their children: see Becker's Charicles E. T. p. 228.

18. **μουσικῇ καὶ γυμναστικῇ**: the two branches of Greek education—the end being to produce a sound mind in a sound body: Pl. Rep. II. 376 E ἔστι δέ που ἡ μὲν (sc. παιδεία) ἐπὶ σώμασι γυμναστική, ἡ δ᾽ ἐπὶ ψυχῇ μουσική. The latter in its wider signification included γράμματα (reading, writing, and arithmetic), κιθάρισις (lyre-playing), and learning by heart passages of the poets, especially Homer. See Becker's Charicles E. T. 226—236.

50 E   19. **καλῶς**. This only commits Socrates to the utility of μουσική and γυμναστική: whether μουσική and γυμναστική were rightly taught is quite another question. It is impossible to believe that Socrates approved of Athenian methods of teaching: for he never wearied of attacking the ignorance of his countrymen, and knowledge according to him could be taught. In the Protagoras (339 foll.) Plato makes him prove by an elaborate caricature of the popular way of expounding the poets that no true education comes from that quarter. Plato himself rejected the popular education both in its actual curriculum and still more in respect of its method: see Rep. VII. 521 C foll.

εἶεν: see on 47 B above.

20. **ἐξετράφης**: ἐξ- signifies that Socrates was no longer a child: so Ar. Nub. 1380 ὠναίσχυντέ, σ᾽ ἐξέθρεψα.

21. **καὶ ἔκγονος καὶ δοῦλος**: Cron compares Hdt. VII. 104, where Demaratus says of the Lacedaemonians ἐλεύθεροι γὰρ ἐόντες οὐ πάντα ἐλεύθεροί εἰσι· ἔπεστι γάρ σφι δεσπότης νόμος. See also Pl. Legg. III. 700 A οὐκ ἦν—ἡμῖν ἐπὶ τῶν παλαιῶν νόμων ὁ δῆμός τινων κύριος, ἀλλὰ τρόπον τινὰ ἑκὼν ἐδούλευε τοῖς νόμοις.

22. **αὐτός τε καὶ οἱ σοὶ πρόγονοι**: Socrates is, so to speak, δοῦλος κἀκ δούλων. With this form of expression compare Apol. 42 A δίκαια πεπονθὼς ἐγὼ ἔσομαι ὑφ᾽ ὑμῶν, αὐτός τε καὶ οἱ υἱεῖς.

23. **ἆρ᾽ ἐξ ἴσου—καὶ ἡμῖν** = 'do you think that your rights are on a level with ours?' (Church): καί=atque, as in pariter atque. The καί after ἡμῖν is explanatory, as in 50 D, line 11.

25. **ἢ πρὸς μὲν ἄρα—πρὸς δὲ τὴν πατρίδα ἄρα**. An *a fortiori* argument: you may not retaliate on your parent or your master:

how much less upon your country and her laws ! Compare Apol.
28 E δεινὰ ἂν εἴην εἰργασμένος—εἰ ὅτε μέν με οἱ ἄρχοντες ἔταττον—
τότε μὲν οὗ ἐκεῖνοι ἔταττον ἔμενον—, τοῦ δὲ θεοῦ τάττοντος—φιλο-
σοφοῦντά με δεῖν ζῆν—, ἐνταῦθα δὲ—λίποιμι τὴν τάξιν : see my note
on the passage. Here, as usual, ἄρα expresses surprise: the presence
of ἄρα in both clauses makes the antithesis more pointed, and in-
creases the rhetorical effect : Cron compares Prot. 325 B—C τὰ μὲν
ἄλλα ἄρα τοὺς υἱεῖς διδάσκονται—, ἐφ' ᾧ δὲ ἥ τε ζημία θάνατος—
καὶ πρὸς τῷ θανάτῳ χρημάτων τε δημεύσεις καὶ ὡς ἔπος εἰπεῖν ξυλλήβδην
τῶν οἴκων ἀνατροπαί, ταῦτα δ' ἄρα οὐ διδάσκονται. The position
of σοι between the preposition and its noun is noteworthy : it is the
less remarkable, because σοι τὸν πατέρα is nearly equivalent to σὸν
πατέρα : cf. Eur. Med. 324 μὴ πρός σε γονάτων : and the well-known
" Lydia dic per omnes te deos oro" of Hor. Carm. I. 8. 1.

26. οὐκ ἐξ ἴσου ἦν : the imperfect implies that Socrates' father
is dead. οὐκ goes closely with ἐξ ἴσου : beware of taking it as=
nonne ?

27. εἴ σοι ὢν ἐτύγχανεν =' if you had chanced to have one'. It
is not necessary to supply οὐκ ἂν ἐξ ἴσου ἦν τὸ δίκαιον : οὐκ ἐξ ἴσου ἦν
is the apodosis, for Greek (like Latin) prefers the more direct and
dogmatic mode of expression (ἦν, erat, rather than ἦν ἄν, esset) :
Goodwin MT. 97.

ὥστε ἄπερ πάσχοις : this explains ἐξ ἴσου : if there had been
equality of rights, Socrates might retaliate: otherwise not. As οὐκ
ἐξ ἴσου forms a single negative idea)(ἔσται sc. ἐξ ἴσου in line 30, we
might have expected ὥστε οὐχ ἄπερ πάσχοις ταῦτα καὶ ἀντιποιεῖν,
just as in 31—33 we have a positive clause with ὥστε to explain the
positive ἔσται ἐξ ἴσου : Plato however prefers to illustrate ἐξ ἴσου,
rather than οὐκ ἐξ ἴσου. Perhaps he was anxious to avoid the
accumulation of negatives.

28. οὔτε κακῶς—ἀλλὰ τοιαῦτα πολλά. This is not epexegetic
of ὥστε—ἀντιποιεῖν (as the editors say) but explains οὐκ ἐξ ἴσου ἦν τὸ
δίκαιον : supply οὐκ ἦν σοι τὸ δίκαιον. κακῶς ἀκούειν (male audire) is
the passive of κακῶς λέγειν (male dicere): so ἀποθνήσκω φεύγω etc.
serve as passives to ἀποκτείνω διώκω etc.: see on Apol. 17 A.

29. τυπτόμενον ἀντιτύπτειν : see the amusing scene in the 51 A
Clouds 1409 foll. Phidippides beats his father Strepsiades, justify-
ing himself in these words : καὶ πρῶτ' ἐρήσομαί σε τουτί· παῖδά μ'
ὄντ' ἔτυπτες ; Στρ. ἔγωγέ σ', εὐνοῶν γε καὶ κηδόμενος. Φειδ. εἰπὲ δή
μοι· οὐ κἀμέ σοι δίκαιόν ἐστιν εὐνοεῖν ὁμοίως, τύπτειν τ', ἐπειδήπερ τόδ'

ἐστὶν εὐνοεῖν, τὸ τύπτειν ; It should be noted that one of the charges
falsely brought against Socrates was that he set sons against their
parents : see Introduction to Apol. p. xxx.

30. **ἔσται σοι** sc. ἐξ ἴσου τὸ δίκαιον. The MSS read ἐξέσται,
which Stallbaum vainly defends. The choice lies between ἐξ ἴσου
ἔσται σοι (Hirschig) and ἔσται σοι (Schanz). I prefer the latter,
both because it changes less, and because I dislike the cadence of
the first : I think Plato, had he chosen to repeat ἐξ ἴσου, would have
omitted σοι. I have added a mark of interrogation after ἔσται σοι :
see on line 32.

31. **ὥστε κτλ.** A result deduced from ἔσται σοι (sc. ἐξ ἴσου).
Note the emphatic σὲ)(ἡμεῖς and in the next line σὺ)(ἡμᾶς : I
follow Göbel and Kral in writing σὲ against σε of the MSS.

32. **καὶ σὺ δέ κτλ.** In place of καὶ σὲ ἡμᾶς—ἐπιχειρεῖν κτλ.
—as we should naturally expect after ὥστε, a vivid question is substituted : compare on 50 D line 10. At the same time a better
antithesis is provided for ἐὰν σὲ ἐπιχειρῶμεν ἡμεῖς ἀπολλύναι, and
the awkwardness of the two accusatives in καὶ σὲ ἡμᾶς κτλ. is
avoided. For καὶ—δέ see following note.

33. **ἐπιχειρήσεις** is of course an independent question : I know
no case of καὶ—δέ in a dependent sentence. This example is instruc-
tive as to the origin of the combination καὶ—δέ = 'and also' : the καί
goes with the intervening words (cf. Aesch. Prom. 972—973 χλιδῶ;
χλιδῶντας ὧδε τοὺς ἐμοὺς ἐγὼ ἐχθροὺς ἴδοιμι· καὶ σὲ δ᾽ ἐν τούτοις
λέγω). The precise force of δέ in this place is difficult to explain.
The editors say that it is used "ad augendam oppositionis gravi-
tatem : pro simplici καὶ σὺ ἡμᾶς dictum est : καὶ σὺ δὲ ἡμᾶς, *usu haud
infrequenti*" (Stallbaum). For this 'not uncommon use' no parallels
are quoted : and I prefer to regard it as the δέ found sometimes in
interrogative sentences, e.g. Prot. 312 A σ ὺ δέ, ἦν δ᾽ ἐγώ, πρὸς θεῶν,
οὐκ ἂν αἰσχύνοιο εἰς τοὺς Ἕλληνας σαυτὸν σοφιστὴν παρέχων;

34. **ταῦτα ποιῶν** sc. ἡμᾶς : cf. 50 E line 24 and note on 44 D
π οιοῦσι δὲ τοῦτο ὅ τι ἂν τύχωσιν. τῇ ἀληθείᾳ is bitterly sarcastic :
Socrates habitually professed ἐπιμελεῖσθαι ἀρετῆς : see Apol. 30 A and
41 E : ἐπιμελεῖσθαι indeed was almost a technical term in Socrates'
preaching : see Xen. Mem. I. 2. 3, 4 etc. Sarcasm is frequently
brought out by adding a qualifying participial clause at the end of a
sentence in this way : e.g. Apol. 34 A εὑρήσετε—πάντας ἐμοὶ βοηθεῖν
ἑτοίμους τῷ διαφθείροντι, τῷ κακὰ ἐργαζομένῳ τοὺς οἰκείους αὐτῶν,
ὥς φασι Μέλητος καὶ Ἄνυτος. It should be noted that the manu-

scripts of Plato often fluctuate between ἐπιμελούμενος and ἐπιμελόμενος : here the Bodleian has ἐπιμελόμενος. On the adverbial phrase
τῇ ἀληθείᾳ see supra note on ὡς ἀληθῶς 46 D.

35. ἢ οὕτως εἶ σοφός. The Bodleian has ἢ without accent:
other MSS read ἤ. ἤ is a far superior reading : for the Laws having
first taken Socrates at his own estimate (ὁ τῇ ἀληθείᾳ τῆς ἀρετῆς
ἐπιμελόμενος) now proceed to take him at other people's. It is clear
from Apol. 18 B that σοφός (like φροντιστής) was almost a nickname
of Socrates. Here of course the word is used with bitter irony, as
indeed it often was in Socrates' time : cf. Meno 75 C τῶν σοφῶν—
καὶ ἐριστικῶν καὶ ἀγωνιστικῶν : Xen. Mem. II. 1 21 Πρόδικος ὁ σοφός.

36. λέληθέν σε ὅτι κτλ : it is implied that the new σοφία (of
which Socrates and the Sophists were thought to be the professors)
tended to lessen the hold of the State upon the individual : see Ar.
Nubes 889—1104.

μητρός τε καὶ πατρός. For the order compare with Cron Prot.
346 A οἷον ἀνδρὶ πολλάκις συμβῆναι μητέρα ἢ πατέρα ἀλλόκοτον ἢ
πατρίδα ἢ ἄλλο τι τῶν τοιούτων : infra 51 C οὔτε μητέρα οὔτε πατέρα. For the sentiment Stallbaum compares Cic. De Off. I. 57
"Cari sunt parentes, cari liberi, propinqui, familiares : sed omnes
omnium caritates patria una complexa est : pro qua quis bonus
dubitet mortem oppetere, si ei sit profuturus?" That one's country
has the first claim on one, and one's family and friends only the
second, was the recognised principle of both Greek and Roman civic
life, during their most flourishing periods. In setting self-study
above political life Socrates was unconsciously preaching a view
whose logical issue amounted to the dissolution of the old life which
it was his aim to restore.

37. τιμιώτερον—καὶ σεμνότερον καὶ ἁγιώτ⸍ρον is a climax :
τίμιος is one of the loftiest epithets that can be applied to τἀνθρώ-
πινα : σεμνός is applied to τὰ θεῖα as well : ἅγιος almost exclusively
to τὰ θεῖα. Translate 'worthier and more august and more sacred'.

38. ἐν μείζονι μοίρᾳ : an elevated and somewhat poetic ex- 51 B
pression : Cron compares Hdt. II. 172 καὶ ἐν οὐδεμιῇ μοίρῃ
μεγάλῃ εἶχον.

39. ἀνθρώποις τοῖς νοῦν ἔχουσι : few and far between : see
Tim. 51 E νοῦ δὲ θεούς (sc. μετέχειν φατέον), ἀνθρώπων δὲ γένος
βραχύ τι.

41. καὶ ἢ πείθειν sc. δεῖ. For πείθειν used absolutely cf. Apol.
35 C διδάσκειν καὶ πείθειν, and supra 48 E πεῖσαι σέ.

43. **ἐάν τε** ('whether') τύπτεσθαι ἐάν τε δεῖσθαι sc. προστάττῃ. This is to explain ἐάν τι προστάττῃ παθεῖν of line 42.

44. **ἐάν τε εἰς πόλεμον κτλ.** ἐάν τε is here='and if': the apodosis is ποιητέον ταῦτα. Socrates had himself fought bravely for his country at Potidaea (432 B.C.), Delium (424 B.C.) and Amphipolis (422 B.C.): see on Apol. 28 E.

46. **καὶ οὐχὶ ὑπεικτέον—λειπτέον τὴν τάξιν.** ὑπείκειν is to give way (it may be slowly) before the enemy, rather than remain to die (ἀποθανούμενον in 45): cf. Rep. VIII. 555 E τὸν ἀεὶ ὑπείκοντα—τιτρώσκοντες. ἀναχωρεῖν is to retreat: Symp. 221 A ἀπὸ Δηλίου φυγῇ ἀνεχώρει τὸ στρατόπεδον. λείπειν τὴν τάξιν suggests the λιποταξίου γ‚αφή. The whole clause is meant to elaborate the idea in ἐάν τε εἰς πόλεμον ἄγῃ τρωθησόμενον ἢ ἀποθανούμενον, ποιητέον ταῦτα.

51 C   49. **ἢ πείθειν** sc. δεῖ, to be supplied from ποιητέον, by a frequent idiom. Stallbaum quotes Gorg. 492 D τὰς μὲν ἐπιθυμίας φῂς οὐ κολαστέον, εἰ μέλλει τις οἷον δεῖ εἶναι, ἐῶντα δὲ αὐτὰς ὡς μεγίστας πληρώσιν αὐταῖς ἀμόθεν γέ ποθεν ἑτοιμάζειν.

50. **βιάζεσθαι.** βιάζεσθαι and πείθειν are often connected or opposed: cf. Gorg. 517 B πείθοντες καὶ βιαζόμενοι ἐπὶ τοῦτο: Rep. VI. 488 D ὅπως ἄρξουσιν ἢ πείθοντες ἢ βιαζόμενοι τὸν ναύκληρον.

CHAPTER XIII.

In this chapter the Laws insist that to remain in Athens is to have pledged oneself to obey them, for emigration is free to all.

2. **ἀληθῆ** is of course predicative, like οὐ δίκαια in the next line.

5. **γεννήσαντες ἐκθρέψαντες παιδεύσαντες**: see on 50 D and on 50 E.

51 D   8. **προαγορεύομεν τῷ ἐξουσίαν πεποιηκέναι**='we proclaim inasmuch as we have given permission'. τῷ βουλομένῳ depends on ἐξουσίαν, and Ἀθηναίων is a partitive genitive after τῷ βουλομένῳ. ἐπειδὰν—νόμους is also to be taken with ἐξουσίαν πεποιηκέναι: the permission is *ipso facto* accorded as soon as the δοκιμασία is past. In line 10 ᾧ ἂν μὴ ἀρέσκωμεν ἡμεῖς depends on ἐξεῖναι, which itself belongs to προαγορεύομεν. The apparent awkwardness of the sen-

tence.is due to the use of ἐξουσίαν without a following infinitive:
but this use is not uncommon in Plato, e.g. Rep. VIII. 557 D where
it is said of democracy πάντα γένη πολιτειῶν ἔχει διὰ τὴν ἐξουσίαν:
ἐξουσία was perhaps one of the familiar watchwords of Athenian
democracy: cf. Thuc. VII. 69 ὑπομιμνήσκων—τῆς—ἀνεπιτάκτου πᾶσιν
—ἐξουσίας.

9. **ἐπειδὰν δοκιμασθῇ.** On attaining the age of 18, every
Athenian was enrolled in the ληξιαρχικὸν γραμματεῖον or register
of his deme, after the usual δοκιμασία or examination. This particular examination was called δοκιμασία εἰς ἄνδρας to distinguish
it from the δοκιμασίαι which the various magistrates had to undergo
before entering upon office. It marked the coming of age of the
young Athenian citizen: but it was not till he was 20 that he took
part in the public assembly and attained the full privileges of
citizenship. From 18 to 20 he had to serve in the περίπολοι or
patrol which guarded the frontiers of Attica. Stallbaum compares
Aeschin. in Timarch. § 18 ἐπειδὰν δ' ἐγγραφῇ εἰς τὸ ληξιαρχικὸν
γραμματεῖον καὶ τοὺς νόμους γνῷ καὶ εἰδῇ τοὺς τῆς πόλεως καὶ
ἤδη δύναται διαλογίζεσθαι τὰ καλὰ καὶ τὰ μὴ κτλ.

11. **λαβόντα,** in spite of the preceding dative ᾧ: cf. Euthyphro 5 A ἆρ' οὖν μοι—κράτιστόν ἐστι μαθητῇ σῷ γενέσθαι καὶ
—αὐτὰ ταῦτα προκαλεῖσθαι αὐτὸν λέγοντα, ὅτι ἔγωγε κτλ. Aesch.
Choeph. 410 πέπαλται δ' αὖτέ μοι φίλον κέαρ τόνδε κλύουσαν
οἶκτον.

12. **καὶ οὐδεὶς—βούληται:** omitted by mistake in B.

14. **ἀποικίαν:** an Athenian colony: contrast μετοικεῖν in 15.
ἀρέσκοιμεν is changed by Madvig (Adv. Crit. I. 369) into ἀρέσκομεν:
but the text is quite sound. εἰ μὴ ἀρέσκοιμεν is the protasis to
the apodosis implied in βούληται—εἰς ἀποικίαν ἰέναι: it explains
why one might wish to emigrate: tr. 'if any of you wants to go
to a colony, supposing we and the State should not satisfy him'.
οὐδεὶς—ἀπαγορεύει, ἐάν—βούληται is the regular form of a general
(as opposed to a particular or special) conditional sentence: Dem.
Ol. 2. 12 ἅπας μὲν λόγος, ἂν ἀπῇ τὰ πράγματα, μάταιόν τι φαίνεται καὶ κενόν: Goodwin MT. 108.

15. **ἐλθών** is not otiose: since μετοικεῖν='be an alien' (μέτοικος):
for μετοικεῖν ἄλλοσε ἐλθών, μετοικῆσαι might have been substituted.
See Goodwin MT. 24.

19. **ὡμολογηκέναι ἔργῳ ἡμῖν**='to have virtually covenanted 51 E
with us'.

21. **γεννηταῖς**: so B, rightly: inferior MSS have γεννήταις. "γεννηταί sunt *genitores:* γεννῆται *gentiles.*—Legg. XI. 928 D διαφοραὶ πατέρων τε πρὸς αὑτῶν παῖδας γίγνονται καὶ παίδων πρὸς γεννητὰς μείζους ἢ χρεών. Contra ib. IX. 878 D τοὺς γεννήτας καὶ τοὺς συγγενεῖς". Wohlrab. MSS however do not always observe this rule.

22. **τροφεῦσι**: Socrates, so to speak, would have paid no τροφεῖα: Rep. VII 520 B.

ὁμολογήσας ἡμῖν πείθεσθαι: ἡμῖν, as Göbel remarks, is to be taken with ὁμολογήσας. For the present πείθεσθαι cf. 50 C ἦ καὶ ταῦτα ὡμολόγητο—ἢ ἐμμένειν ταῖς δίκαις: and infr. 52 D ὡμολογηκέναι πολιτεύεσθαι. In each of these passages Madvig (Adv. Crit. I. 370 note 1) changes the present to the future infinitive, on the ground that ὁμολογῶ με ποιεῖν=confiteor me facere, promitto me facturum=ὁμολογῶ με ποιήσειν (not ποιεῖν). The truth is that ὁμολογεῖν has two meanings, viz. 'to confess', and to 'bargain' or 'promise': and, since the word 'promise' itself implies futurity, it may even in this sense be followed by a present infinitive, although the future is preferred, when the notion of futurity is more prominent. Just so in English we can say 'I promise to do' as well as 'I promise that I will do'. The same distinction holds in my opinion for ἐλπίζω, ἐλπίς ἐστι, προσδοκῶ, ἐπίδοξός εἰμι, οἶμαι, φημί, νομίζω, δοκῶ, εἰκός ἐστι etc. with the present and future infinitive: although Madvig, Cobet, and the stricter school of critics generally insist that the notion of futurity must be expressed by the infinitive as well. See Madvig Adv. Crit. I. 156 foll., Cobet Var. Lect. 97 foll., Rutherford's Babrius p. 13, and on the other hand Kühner Gr. Gr. II. p. 163 ff.

24. **προτιθέντων**: the object is ποιεῖν ἃ ἂν κελεύωμεν. προτιθέναι is to propose some course of action, without, at the same time, excluding an alternative: this is still further brought out in ἀλλ' ἐφιέντων δυοῖν θάτερα κτλ. ἀγρίως ἐπιτάττειν suggests the angry tyrant: Gorg. 510 B τύραννος—ἄγριος καὶ ἀπαίδευτος: Rep. I. 329 C ὥσπερ λυττῶντά τινα καὶ ἄγριον δεσπότην ἀποφυγών. For the asyndeton see on τὰ τοιαῦτα ἐλέγετο 47 A above. I have printed a colon before προτιθέντων as in 49 B.

CHAPTER XIV.

It is here argued that Socrates, if he were to abscond, would more than any other Athenian be guilty of a breach of bargain, because throughout all his life, even during the trial as well as before, he had shewn that Athens was more to him than any other city.

1. **Σώκρατες.** So B: inferior MSS read ὦ Σώκρατες. The 52 A effect of omitting ὦ is to increase the impressiveness, since ὦ Σώκρατες is the regular mode of address: in English we obtain the same effect by exactly the opposite means.

2. **ἐνέξεσθαι** i.q. ἔνοχον ἔσεσθαι.

4. **ἐν τοῖς μάλιστα.** See above on ἐν τοῖς βαρύτατα 43 C.

5. **καθάπτοιντο.** καθάπτεσθαι (in Homer with acc., in Attic with gen.) is 'to fasten on', 'attack': Thuc. VI. 16. 1 ἀνάγκη γὰρ ἐντεῦθεν ἄρξασθαι, ἐπειδή μου Νικίας καθήψατο.

9. **τούτων** refers forward to the clause introduced by ὅτι. 52 B

11. **διαφερόντως**: differently from, i.e. more than : so too διαφέρειν. For the repetition of διαφερόντως in the protasis cf. Apol. 31 D εἰ ἐγὼ πάλαι ἐπεχείρησα πράττειν τὰ πολιτικὰ πράγματα, πάλαι ἂν ἀπολώλη.

13. **ἐπὶ θεωρίαν** = "ad spectandos ludos sollemnes, videlicet Olympicos, Nemeaeos, Isthmios, Pythios, ad quos spectandos ex universa Graecia homines confluebant". Stallbaum.

14. **ἐξῆλθες.** An hypothetical clause οὐ γὰρ ἄν—ἐπεδήμεις is now followed by an unconditional statement of fact. After ἐξῆλθες in inferior MSS and in the margin of B are found the words ὅτι μὴ ἅπαξ εἰς Ἰσθμόν. The interpretation (for such it probably is) was already in the text used by Athenaᵉus: see V. 216 B ἐν δὲ τῷ Κρίτωνι,—Πλάτων οὐδὲ ποιήσασθαί ποτε ἀποδημίαν τὸν Σωκράτη ἔξω τῆς εἰς Ἰσθμὸν πορείας. Nowhere else in Plato do we find any mention of such a journey, and at least one passage seems distinctly to deny it: Phaedr. 230 C ἐκ τοῦ ἄστεος οὔτ' εἰς τὴν ὑπερορίαν ἀποδημεῖς οὔτ' ἔξω τείχους ἔμοιγε δοκεῖς τὸ παράπαν ἐξιέναι. Diogenes Laertius seems to have found the story in Favorinus, but not in Plato: he also attributes to Aristotle (no doubt wrongly) a statement to the effect that Socrates visited Delphi as well: see II. 5. 23 καὶ Πυθώδε ἐλθεῖν Ἀριστοτέλης φησίν· ἀλλὰ καὶ εἰς Ἰσθμόν, ὡς Φαβωρῖνος ἐν τῷ πρώτῳ τῶν ἀπομνημονευμάτων.

εἰ μή ποι στρατευσόμενος: viz. at Potidaea, Delium, and Amphi-polis: see on 51 B above, and Apol. 28 E.

15. ἀποδημίαν. Cron remarks that οὐδεμίαν is omitted after ἀποδημίαν for the sake of euphony.

16. ὥσπερ οἱ ἄλλοι ἄνθρωποι: 'Philosophi praesertim'. Forster. Cf. Hdt. I. 30, where Croesus says to Solon: περὶ σέο λόγος ἀπῖκται πολλός—, ὡς φιλοσοφέων γῆν πολλὴν—ἐπελήλυθας.

ἐπιθυμία σε ἄλλης πόλεως—ἔλαβεν εἰδέναι. By an idiom analo-gous to οἶδά σε τίς εἶ the object of the infinitive εἰδέναι is made de-pendent on the word (ἐπιθυμία) upon which the infinitive itself depends: cf. Gorg. 513 E ἐπιχειρητέον ἐστὶ τῇ πόλει καὶ τοῖς πολίταις θεραπεύειν: Rep. IV. 443 B εὐθὺς ἀρχόμενοι τῆς πόλεως οἰκίζειν. So in Latin quarum potiendi spe (Cic. de Fin. I. 60).

52 C   19. ἠροῦ—ὡμολόγεις—ἐποιήσω: for the combination of imper-fect and aorist see on 50 D καὶ δι' ἡμῶν ἐλάμβανεν τὴν μητέρα σου ὁ πατὴρ καὶ ἐφύτευσέν σε. With ὡμολογεῖς πολιτεύσεσθαι contrast 51 E ὁμολογήσας ἡμῖν πείθεσθαι: see note *in loc.*

20. τά τε ἄλλα καὶ = 'and in particular'. The τά τε ἄλλα goes grammatically with ὡμολόγεις, not with πολιτεύσεσθαι (Cron) or with καὶ ἐπολιτεύου to be supplied from it (Stallbaum, Wohlrab, Göbel): to beget children in the city was virtually to *pledge oneself* (ὁμολο-γεῖν) to obey its laws.

21. ἔτι τοίνυν. τοίνυν = 'moreover', as often in Plato and the orators. Apol. 33 E.

22. φυγῆς τιμήσασθαι = 'to propose the penalty of exile'. Cf. Apol. 37 C ἀλλὰ δὴ φυγῆς τιμήσωμαι; ἴσως γὰρ ἄν μοι τούτου τιμήσαιτε. In an ἀγὼν τιμητός, like Socrates' trial, it was the duty of the accused, should he be found guilty, to propose a counter penalty to that demanded by the prosecutor. Socrates proposed a fine of 30 minae: see Apol. 38 B.

24. ἐκαλλωπίζου ὡς οὐκ ἀγανακτῶν: viz. in Apol. 37 C—38 A. So Theaet. 195 D καλλωπιζόμενος ὡς τι εὑρηκότων ἡμῶν καλόν.

25. τεθνάναι: see on τεθνάναι in 43 C above.

26. λόγους αἰσχύνει: quite different from ἐπὶ λόγοις αἰσχύνει: here the λόγοι are personified. Cf. Charm. 169 C ᾐσχύνετο τοὺς παρόντας.

27. ἐντρέπει. 'Turn to' naturally passes into 'give heed to', 'regard': so advertere in Latin.

52 D   28. διαφθεῖραι: because the Laws are personified: see Introd. p. vii.

29. **ἀποδιδράσκειν** is the regular word to denote the running away of a slave: see on 50 A above.

30. **ξυνέθου πολιτεύεσθαι**: see on ὁμολογήσας ἡμῖν πείθεσθαι in 51 E.

33. **ἔργῳ** belongs to ὡμολογηκέναι: see 51 E ἤδη φαμὲν τοῦτον ὡμολογηκέναι ἔργῳ ἡμῖν ἃ ἂν ἡμεῖς κελεύωμεν ποιήσειν. ἀλλ' οὐ λόγῳ is bracketed by Göbel, after Hoenebeek : but the words serve to emphasize ἔργῳ—'with deeds, not with words'. It is implied that a verbal compact is less binding than one in which deeds take the place of words. The opposition of λόγος and ἔργον is familiar from Thucydides. For ἀλλά see note on 47 B.

34. **ἄλλο τι ἤ** = 'nonne': supra on 50 A. ὁμολογῶμεν is a deliberative conjunctive: like imperatival expressions generally, the deliberative conjunctive can be used in subordinate as well as in principal clauses: as here the full construction is ἄλλο τί ἐστιν ἤ (=quam, not aut) ὁμολογῶμεν. Cf. Crat. 425 D εἰ μὴ ἄρα δή—ἀπαλλαγῶμεν i.e. 'unless perhaps we are to get off'. See Postgate in Proceedings of the Cambridge Philological Society, Vol. III. Part I. pp. 50—55.

37. **ἂν φαῖεν**: for the position of ἄν compare Phaed. 87 A τί οὖν, ἂν φαίη ὁ λόγος, ἔτι ἀπιστεῖς ;

38. **ἡμᾶς αὐτούς**. αὐτούς seems to emphasize ἡμᾶς: there is no reflexive meaning. Cron compares Phaed. 79 A ἄλλο τι ἡμῶν αὐτῶν τὸ μὲν σῶμά ἐστι, τὸ δὲ ψυχή; For αὐτούς Göbel conjectures σαυτοῦ, comparing 54 C : at first sight there seems no occasion for the unusually emphatic mode of expression. I think the meaning is 'bargains made actually with us': bad as it always is to break a bargain, it is still worse when the party to it is one's country: cf. 51 A—C μητρός τε καὶ πατρὸς καὶ τῶν ἄλλων προγόνων ἀπάντων τιμιώτερόν ἐστιν ἡ πατρὶς κτλ.

41. **ἔτεσιν ἑβδομήκοντα** : Socrates was born in 469 B.C.   52 E
ἐν οἷς ἐξῆν σοι ἀπιέναι: hardly accurate: see 51 D.

44. **ἃς δὴ ἑκάστοτε φῂς εὐνομεῖσθαι** : as in Xen. Mem. III. 5. 15—16 and IV. 4. 15, and often in Plato e.g. Prot. 342 A foll. and Rep. VIII. 544 C ἥ τε ὑπὸ τῶν πολλῶν ἐπαινουμένη, ἡ Κρητική τε καὶ Λακωνικὴ αὕτη· καὶ δευτέρα κτλ. What Socrates most admired in Crete and Sparta was their implicit obedience to the law : they formed the best possible illustration of his principle—τὸ δίκαιον is τὸ νόμιμον: see Introd. p. xiii. ἑκάστοτε sc. quotiescumque de iis loqueris (Stallbaum).

45. **οὐδὲ τῶν βαρβαρικῶν.** Socrates had occasional glimpses of a world beyond the pale of Hellenism, if we may trust Phaed. 78 A πολλὴ μὲν ἡ Ἑλλάς—πολλὰ δὲ καὶ τὰ τῶν βαρβάρων γένη, οὓς πάντας χρὴ διερευνᾶσθαι ζητοῦντας τοιοῦτον ἐπῳδόν. It should be noted that οὐδέ goes closely with οὐδεμίαν : it of course has nothing to do with the preceding οὔτε.

53 A   46. **ἐλάττω—ἀπεδήμησας :** comparative of ὀλίγα—ἀπεδήμησας. For the statement itself see note on ἐξῆλθες in 52 B above.

47. **ἀνάπηροι** are "quicumque carent vel membro aliquo et parte corporis vel certe eius usu". Fischer. For the ἀνα- cf. ἀναπλέως, ἀναπιμπλάναι in their medical sense : see on Apol. 32 C.

49. **δῆλον ὅτι :** adverbial : ὅτι as in εὖ οἶδ᾽ ὅτι. The adverb is placed for emphasis at the end of the sentence as εἰκότως is so often in Demosthenes : just so in Symp. 195 B φεύγων φυγῇ τὸ γῆρας, ταχὺ ὂν δῆλον ὅτι· θᾶττον γοῦν τοῦ δέοντος ἡμῖν προσέρχεται.

50. **ἄνευ νόμων** goes closely with πόλις : 'a city without laws'. The other meaning which suggests itself—'who could like a state without liking her laws?'—cannot be got out of the Greek : ἄνευ νόμων cannot = ἄνευ τοῦ νόμους ἀρέσκειν. The reasoning is—no one could like a state which had no laws : you like your state, therefore you like her laws. Schanz (after Hirschig) brackets δῆλον ὅτι—ἄνευ νόμων : but the clause contains a valuable and strictly relevant idea, viz. that a πόλις ἄνευ νόμων is a πόλις ἄπολις.

νῦν δὲ δή = 'but now forsooth'. οὐκ ἐμμένεις is better than οὐκ ἐμμενεῖς (so Schanz with the second hand in B): cf. πράττεις and παραβαίνεις in 52 D.

51. **ἐὰν ἡμῖν γε πείθῃ** = 'yes, if you take our advice'. For the form of expression cf. 53 E οὐδείς ὃς ἐρεῖ; ἴσως, ἂν μή τινα λυπῇς : see also 53 C—D and 54 B.

καὶ οὐ καταγέλαστός γε ἔσει = 'and at least you will escape being laughed at'. This reappears in 53 D. τὸ καταγέλαστον makes one καταγελᾶν : τὸ γελοῖον only γελᾶν. Hence γελοῖον often = 'funny' 'amusing'. Symp. 189 B (loquitur Aristophanes) φοβοῦμαι περὶ τῶν μελλόντων ῥηθήσεσθαι, οὔ τι μὴ γελοῖα εἴπω, τοῦτο μὲν γὰρ ἂν κέρδος εἴη καὶ τῆς ἡμετέρας μούσης ἐπιχώριον, ἀλλὰ μὴ καταγέλαστα.

CHAPTER XV.

The Laws now reply in detail to the arguments of Crito: see
Chapters III—v and compare Introduction pp. viii—ix. Escape will
bring danger on his friends, misery and disgrace upon himself, and
to say the least will leave his children in no way better provided.

1. σκόπει γὰρ δή 'Just consider'. γάρ is introductory: see
on 44 A.

παραβὰς καὶ ἐξαμαρτάνων. Note the difference of tense: an
ἁμαρτία remains so till it is expiated. Cf. ἠδίκει in 50 C, where see
note. ταῦτα in ταῦτα παραβάς is not 'these duties' (Göbel), but
'these transgressions': a cognate accusative.

4. σου οἱ ἐπιτήδειοι is preferred to οἱ σοὶ ἐπιτήδειοι for reasons 53 B
of sound, and also perhaps because ἐπιτήδειοι is still felt to be an
adjective.

5. καὶ αὐτοὶ φεύγειν = 'et ipsi exulare': sc. as well as you:
καὶ στερηθῆναι τῆς πόλεως i.q. ἄτιμοι γενέσθαι sc. by banishment.
On στερηθῆναι see above, note on 44 B. The Laws here reply to
Crito's pleading in 44 E and 45 E.

6. σχεδόν τι 'pretty nearly', propemodum. σχεδόν τι, ὡς ἔπος
εἰπεῖν, and ἔμβραχυ all mean much the same: the first generally goes
with adjectives, the second with οὐδείς or πᾶς; the third is found
only with relatives (ἔμβραχυ περὶ ὅτου ἂν βούληται Gorg. 457 A).

7. πρῶτον μέν: the second alternative comes infra in D ἀλλ' ἐκ
μὲν τούτων τῶν τόπων ἀπαρεῖς, ἥξεις δὲ εἰς Θετταλίαν κτλ. See
on πρῶτον μέν in 50 D.

9. Θήβαζε. For Θήβασδε: ζ was in fact pronounced dz: see
Gustav Meyer, Griechische Grammatik² p. 219. So Ἀθήναζε θύραζε
χαμᾶζε. Note the double accent in Μέγαράδε (so Bekker, Cron,
Schanz, Göbel: Wohlrab however reads Μεγάραδε and Kral Με-
γαράδε): δε is enclitic. The constitution of Thebes and Megara was
oligarchical: hence εὐνομοῦνται γὰρ ἀμφότεραι is said (not without
a touch of sarcasm) from Socrates' point of view.

10. πολέμιος ἥξεις τῇ τούτων πολιτείᾳ. Because even though
you approve of their constitution, you have violated your own, and
may violate theirs next, now that you have ceased to believe that
δίκαιον is νόμιμον. τούτων is masculine.

12. ὑποβλέψονταί σε = 'will eye you askance'. So in Symp.
220 B οἱ δὲ στρατιῶται ὑπέβλεπον αὐτὸν ὡς καταφρονοῦντα σφῶν.

ὑπο- is 'from under the eyebrows': i.e. with a scowling expression (ταυρηδὸν ὑποβλέψας Phaed. 117 B), or sometimes furtively, of the stolen glances of lovers: see L. and S. s. v.

διαφθορέα τῶν νόμων: see on 50 B and Introd. p. vii.

13. βεβαιώσεις τοῖς δικασταῖς τὴν δόξαν ὥστε δοκεῖν. τοῖς δικασταῖς is a dativus commodi. For τὴν δόξαν ὥστε δοκεῖν see on 44 C τίς ἂν αἰσχίων εἴη ταύτης δόξα ἢ δοκεῖν κτλ.

53 C   15. σφόδρα που—διαφθορεὺς εἶναι: since it is easier διαφθείρειν ἀνοήτους ἀνθρώπους than reasonable laws. νόμων and ἀνθρώπων are opposed. The indictment of Socrates is to be found in Apol. 24 B Σωκράτη φησὶν ἀδικεῖν τούς τε νέους διαφθείροντα καὶ θεοὺς οὓς ἡ πόλις νομίζει οὐ νομίζοντα, ἕτερα δὲ δαιμόνια καινά.

18. κοσμιωτάτους: κόσμιος is ὁ κόσμον ἔχων Gorg. 506 E.

19. ἢ πλησιάσεις τούτοις. τούτοις = τοῖς κοσμιωτάτοις: whence ἀναισχυντήσεις.

20. τίνας λόγους;—ἢ οὕσπερ. More vivid than τοὺς αὐτοὺς λόγους οὕσπερ. B has ἦ: so Cron and Göbel. Schanz and Wohlrab read ἤ with some MS authority. ἦ = Latin -ne? ἤ = Latin an?: see on Apol. 26 B.

21. ὡς ἡ ἀρετὴ—πλείστου ἄξιον: see Apol. 30 A—B, and note.

53 D   23. ἄσχημον ἂν φανεῖσθαι. On ἄν with future participle see Goodwin MT. p. 60. Hirschig reads ἀναφανεῖσθαι.

τὸ τοῦ Σωκράτους πρᾶγμα = 'Socrates and everything about him'. So οἱ περὶ Ἄνυτον = 'Anytus and those with him': Apol. 18 B. There is some contempt in the expression: cf. Hipp. Maior 286 E φαῦλον γὰρ ἂν εἴη τὸ ἐμὸν πρᾶγμα καὶ ἰδιωτικόν. Χρῆμα is used in much the same way, only with still more contempt, e.g. Rep. VIII. 567 E ἦ μακάριον, ἦν δ' ἐγώ, λέγεις τυράννου χρῆμα. Weariness and disgust are expressed by a similar phrase in the first line of the Clouds: ὦ Ζεῦ βασιλεῦ, τὸ χρῆμα τῶν νυκτῶν ὅσον.

24. οἴεσθαί γε χρή: a way of answering one's own question: so infra 54 B.

25. ἀπαρεῖς: Socrates as an exile moving from city to city: cf. Apol. 37 D καλὸς οὖν οὖν ἄν μοι ὁ βίος εἴη ἐξελθόντι, τηλικῷδε ἀνθρώπῳ ἄλλην ἐξ ἄλλης πόλεως ἀμειβομένῳ καὶ ἐξελαυνομένῳ ζῆν. The Laws are now replying to Crito's proposal in 45 C.

26. πλείστη ἀταξία καὶ ἀκολασία. ἀταξία is the opposite of κοσμιότης: ἀκολασία of σωφροσύνη: see Gorg. 506 D—507 A. Thessaly and Macedonia were almost proverbial for licence and debauchery: see (for Thessaly) Xen. Mem. I. 2. 24 Κριτίας—φυγὼν εἰς

Θετταλίαν ἐκεῖ συνῆν ἀνθρώποις ἀνομίᾳ μᾶλλον ἢ δικαιοσύνῃ χρωμένοις:
and Theopompus ap. Athen. XII. 527 ζῶσιν οἱ μὲν σὺν ταῖς ὀρχηστρίσι καὶ ταῖς αὐλητρίσι διατρίβοντες, οἱ δ' ἐν κύβοις καὶ πότοις καὶ ταῖς τοιαύταις ἀκολασίαις διημερεύοντες, καὶ μᾶλλον σπουδάζουσιν ὅπως ὄψων παντοδαπῶν τὰς τραπέζας παραθήσονται πλήρεις ἢ τὸν αὑτῶν βίον παρασχήσονται κεκοσμημένον.

27. **ὡς γελοίως**: see on καταγέλαστος in 53 A.

28. **ἀπεδίδρασκες**: the pictorial imperfect. σκευή is dress or apparel of some kind, generally unusual, as for instance the dress of an actor.

29. **ἢ διφθέραν λαβὼν ἢ ἄλλα**: two kinds of σκευή are specified. The διφθέρα was a shepherd's skin coat.

30. **ἐνσκευάζεσθαι**=induere.

καὶ τὸ σχῆμα μεταλλάξας: καὶ corresponds to τε in σκευήν τέ τινα (line 28). The clause refers to personal disguises not connected with dress. B has καταλλάξας corrected to μεταλλάξας in the margin. μεταλλάσσειν='to change': καταλλάσσειν=(1) 'to exchange' (2) 'to reconcile'.

33. **οὕτως αἰσχρῶς** goes with ζῆν and is explained by νόμους 53 E τοὺς μεγίστους παραβάς.

34. **οὐδεὶς ὃς ἐρεῖ**: with omission of the copula as in οὐδεὶς ὅστις οὔ.

35. **ἀκούσει** serves as passive to ἐρεῖς: see on 50 E. εἰ δὲ μή =alioquin: cf. (with Forster) Phaed. 91 c ἐὰν μέν τι ὑμῖν δοκῶ ἀληθὲς λέγειν, συνομολογήσατε, εἰ δὲ μή, παντὶ λόγῳ ἀντιτείνετε.

36. **ὑπερχόμενος**='cringing to', 'fawning on'. In this sense (=θωπεύω, πρὸς χάριν ὁμιλῶ) ὑπέρχομαι may be used outside pres. Indicative in good Attic: when='go under', then like ἔρχομαι and its compounds generally, it supplies the other parts from εἶμι (ᾖα, ἴω, ἴοιμι, ἴθι, ἰέναι, ἰών, fut. εἶμι). Cobet, Variae Lectiones pp. 34, 307.

βιώσει. "Verbum ζῆν habet ἀττικιστί has formas ζῶ, βιώσομαι, ἐβίων, βεβίωκα, βεβίωταί μοι. βιῶ et ἐβίουν nemo dicit, sed ζῶ et ἔζων ἔζης ἔζη. βιοῖ et similia Ionica sunt. ζήσω apud Atticos *semel* et *iterum* comparet." Cobet, Var. Lect. p. 610.

37. **δουλεύων** is not otiose, as Stallbaum points out: for the δοῦλος is a degree below the κόλαξ.

τί ποιῶν ἢ εὐωχούμενος. τί=τί ἄλλο: cf. Meno 86 E εἰ μή τι οὖν, ἀλλὰ σμικρόν γέ μοι τῆς ἀρχῆς χάλασον. Rep. VI. 509 C καὶ μηδαμῶς γ', ἔφη, παύσῃ, εἰ μή τι, ἀλλὰ—διεξιών. For εὐωχούμενος used in connection with the luxury of the north cf. Ar. Ran. 83—

85: Ἀγάθων δὲ ποῦ 'στιν; ἀπολιπὼν ἔμ' οἴχεται, ἀγαθὸς ποιητὴς καὶ ποθεινὸς τοῖς φίλοις. ποῖ γῆς ὁ τλήμων; ἐς μακάρων εὐωχίαν: Agathon had settled at the court of Archelaus king of Macedon. Schanz brackets and Kral rejects ἐν Θετταλίᾳ: but there is rhetorical force in the double mention of Thessaly at the end of the two clauses: see on 53 D line 26.

38. ὥσπερ ἐπὶ δεῖπνον—Θετταλίαν; added with bitter scorn to explain the Θετταλῶν εὐωχία.

54 A   40. ἀλλὰ δή: alluding to Crito's plea in 45 C—D. ἀλλὰ δή is like 'at enim' 'oh but', and introduces a counter-argument: see Protag. 338 C ἀλλὰ δὴ βελτίονα ἡμῶν αἱρήσεσθε τῇ μὲν ἀληθείᾳ.— ἀδύνατον ὑμῖν, ὥστε Πρωταγόρου τοῦδε σοφώτερόν τινα ἑλέσθαι· εἰ δὲ αἱρήσεσθε κτλ. In accordance with this and other examples, I have printed a full stop after παιδεύσῃς: the other editors take the sentence as interrogative.

42. τί δέ;=quid vero? Note the emphatic place of εἰς Θετταλίαν: Thessaly had an evil name: see on 53 D.

43. ἵνα καὶ τοῦτο ἀπολαύσωσιν: τοῦτο=τὸ ξένοι εἶναι. ἀπολαύειν has ironical force: the word is ordinarily used of something good. So in Eur. Phoen. 1204—5 Κρέων δ' ἔοικε τῶν ἐμῶν νυμφευμάτων τῶν τ' Οἰδίπου δύστηνος ἀπολαῦσαι κακῶν κτλ. ἀπολαύω is construed generally with gen. of the object from which the enjoyment is derived, except where that object is a neuter pronoun: inferior MSS here read τοῦτό σου.

44. οὔ i.e. οὐκ ἔσται. παιδευθήσομαι is used as well as παιδεύσομαι in the passive sense: θρέψομαι is however better than τραφήσομαι.

45. ξυνόντος. ξυνεῖναι and ξυνουσία are regularly used in Plato of the relation between teacher and pupil, e.g. Gorg. 515 B τίνα φήσεις βελτίω πεποιηκέναι ἄνθρωπον τῇ συνουσίᾳ τῇ σῇ; Hence the τόκος ἐν καλῷ of Symp. 206 B.

46. ἐπιμελήσονται: see on 51 A line 34 above. Schanz brackets ἐπιμελήσονται here, reading οἱ σοὶ αὐτῶν πότερον κτλ.: but the sentence is spoken from Socrates' point of view.

54 B   49. σοι of course goes with ἐπιτηδείων. For οἴεσθαί γε χρή in the next line see on 53 D.

CHAPTER XVI.

The Laws conclude their appeal by asking Socrates to think of the future world as well as this : see Introd. pp. viii and xvi.

2. **τροφεῦσι** : see 51 A. Meiser reads τοῖς σοῖς γεννηταῖς καὶ τοῖς σοῖς τροφεῦσι.

3. **πρὸ τοῦ δικαίου** after πλείονος, as after other comparatives in Phaed. 99 A εἰ μὴ δικαιότερον ᾤμην καὶ κάλλιον εἶναι πρὸ τοῦ φεύγειν τε καὶ ἀποδιδράσκειν ὑπέχειν τῇ πόλει δίκην ἥν τιν' ἂν τάττῃ. Cobet needlessly rejects πρό : see Wohlrab in Fleckeisen's Jahrb. for 1876 p. 126. For δίκαιον see note on 45 C ἔτι δὲ οὐδὲ δίκαιον above.

4. **ἵνα εἰς "Αιδου ἐλθών** : the belief in a future life is expressed more dogmatically here than in the Apology : see 40 C foll. Compare Introd. p. xvi.

5. **τοῖς ἐκεῖ ἄρχουσιν** : compare Gorg. 526 D—E ἐγὼ μὲν οὖν— ὑπὸ τούτων τῶν λόγων πέπεισμαι καὶ σκοπῶ ὅπως ἀποφανοῦμαι τῷ κριτῇ ὡς ὑγιεστάτην τὴν ψυχήν—καὶ ὀνειδίζω σοι ὅτι οὐχ οἷός τ' ἔσει σαυτῷ βοηθῆσαι, ὅταν ἡ δίκη σοι ᾖ καὶ ἡ κρίσις ἣν νῦν δὴ ἔλεγον, ἀλλὰ ἐλθὼν παρὰ τὸν δικαστὴν τὸν τῆς Αἰγίνης υἱόν, ἐπειδάν σου ἐπιλαβόμενος ἄγῃ, χασμήσει καὶ ἰλιγγιάσεις οὐδὲν ἧττον ἢ ἐγὼ ἐνθάδε σὺ ἐκεῖ.

7. **οὐδὲ δικαιότερον οὐδὲ ὁσιώτερον.** οὐδέ joins ἄμεινον to δικαιότερον : οὔτε in line 6 corresponds to οὔτε in line 8. δίκαιον is τὸ προσῆκον περὶ ἀνθρώπους : ὅσιον, τὸ προσῆκον περὶ θεούς : see Gorg. 507 B.

8. **οὐδὲ ἄλλῳ.** οὐδέ joins σοι in line 6 to ἄλλῳ. ἐκεῖσε of the future world : see on Apol. 40 E ὡς ἄρα ἐκεῖ εἰσιν ἅπαντες οἱ τεθνεῶτες : cf. τοῖς ἐκεῖ ἄρχουσιν in line 5 and ἐκεῖ in C line 16.

10. **οὐχ ὑφ' ἡμῶν τῶν νόμων, ἀλλὰ ὑπὸ ἀνθρώπων** : the ἄνθρωποι are the δικασταί, falsely so called : see Apol. 24 D—E. For the full significance of this sentence see Introduction pp. x—xi : and cf. note on 49 B οὐδὲ ἀδικούμενον ἄρα ἀνταδικεῖν. Hence ἀνταδικήσας and ἀντικακουργήσας in 11 and 12 have for their object not the laws, but the δικασταί.   54 C

11. **οὕτως αἰσχρῶς** goes with ἐξέλθῃς and is explained by the two participles that follow. There is an allusion to 49 B—D.

13. **παραβὰς καὶ κακὰ ἐργασάμενος** : these participles explain ἀνταδικήσας τε καὶ ἀντικακουργήσας.

14. **οὓς ἥκιστα ἔδει, σαυτόν τε κτλ.** Note the emphatic place of σαυτόν : oneself is the last person one should injure. Compare Apol. 37 B πεπεισμένος δὴ ἐγὼ μηδένα ἀδικεῖν πολλοῦ γε δέω ἐμαυτόν γε ἀδικήσειν. Socrates' philosophy was egoism : see Introd. pp. xii—xiii. σαυτόν τε καὶ φίλους καὶ πατρίδα καὶ ἡμᾶς sums up the argument of Chapters XI—XV.

16. **οἱ ἐν Ἅιδου νόμοι :** Cron refers to Soph. Antig. 450 foll. οὐ γάρ τί μοι Ζεὺς ἦν ὁ κηρύξας τάδε, οὐδ' ἡ ξύνοικος τῶν κάτω θεῶν Δίκη τοιούσδ' ἐν ἀνθρώποισιν ὥρισεν νόμους.

54 D   19. **μή σε πείσῃ :** Goodwin MT. p. 181.

CHAPTER XVII.

Socrates concludes by giving his verdict in favour of the laws and constitution of Athens.   Introd. pp. xi and xvi—xvii.

1. **ὦ φίλε ἑταῖρε Κρίτων.** There is pathos and sympathy in this unusually long mode of address : Cobet and Naber utterly spoil the passage by omitting Κρίτων : Göbel omits ἑταῖρε.

2. **οἱ κορυβαντιῶντες τῶν αὐλῶν δοκοῦσιν ἀκούειν.** The Corybantes were priests of Cybele whose worship was attended with much clamour of dancing and music on the flute.   Lambinus aptly compares Hor. Epist. I. 1. 7 'est mihi purgatam crebro qui personet aurem'.   Göbel omits δοκοῦσιν ἀκούειν, but the text as it stands is far more impressive.   Just so the demonstrative is repeated in αὕτη ἡ ἠχὴ τούτων τῶν λόγων, and in the last line of the chapter : πράττωμεν ταύτῃ, ἐπειδὴ ταύτῃ ὁ θεὸς ὑφηγεῖται.

5. **βομβεῖ καὶ ποιεῖ μὴ δύνασθαι τῶν ἄλλων ἀκούειν.** Socrates might have said much the same of his δαιμόνιον σημεῖον : compare Apol. 40 A—B.   I think Plato meant to suggest that the pleading of the Laws coincided with the voice of the divine sign : see Introd. p. xvi.

6. **ὅσα γε τὰ νῦν ἐμοὶ δοκοῦντα.** Socrates' diffidence is characteristic : cf. Rep. VI. 506 E πλέον γάρ μοι φαίνεται ἢ κατὰ τὴν παροῦσαν ὁρμὴν ἐφικέσθαι τοῦ γε δοκοῦντος ἐμοὶ τὰ νῦν ('what is after all only my present opinion').   Compare Gorg. 527 A and Phaed. 85 C—D.   For the syntax cf. 46 E ὅσα γε τἀνθρώπεια.

11. **ἐπειδὴ ταύτῃ ὁ θεὸς ὑφηγεῖται.** Compare the words with which the Apology concludes (42 A) ἄδηλον παντὶ πλὴν ἢ τῷ θεῷ. The voice of the Laws seems to Socrates to be the voice of God : his divine sign would not allow him to escape.   See Introd., p. xvi.

APPENDIX.

List of Deviations from the Bodleian.

As the text of this edition is based upon Schanz's collation of the Bodleian, it may be convenient to note the most important deviations from this MS. When I differ from Schanz and the other editors, it will generally be found that I have kept more closely to the MS reading: most of the cases in which I have departed from it are discussed in the notes. Whenever I have adopted a reading which may be traced to some member of the second family of MSS, best represented by T=Bekker's t, I have signified this by writing fam. sec. after the reading in question.

	Readings of B.	The present edition.
43 A	πρωὶ	πρῲ
	εὐεργέτηται	εὐηργέτηται
43 B	εὐδαιμόνισα	ηὐδαιμόνισα
43 C	πρωὶ	πρῲ
	χαλεπὴν καὶ βαρεῖαν ("καὶ βαρεῖαν punctis notatum" Sch.)	χαλεπὴν (fam. sec.)
43 D	δοκεῖν μέν μοι ἥξειν ("ν verbi δοκεῖν punctis notata in B." Sch.)	δοκεῖ μέν μοι ἥξειν (fam. sec.)
44 B	οὐδεμία ξυμφορά	οὐ μία ξυμφορά (fam. sec.)
44 C	σῴζειν	σῴζειν
44 E	ἄλλο τι πρὸς τούτους (corrected by second hand)	ἄλλο τι πρὸς τούτοις
45 A	φοβῇ	φοβεῖ
45 E	πεπρᾶχθαι (corrected by second hand)	πεπρᾶχθαι
	ὡς εἰσῆλθεν	ὡς εἰσῆλθες (fam. sec.)
	τὸ τελευταῖον δήπου	τὸ τελευταῖον δή (fam. sec.)
46 A	πεπράχθαι (corr. sec. manus)	πεπρᾶχθαι
46 D	ἄλλως ἕνεκα λόγου	ἄλλως [ἕνεκα λόγου]
	νυνδὴ	νῦν δὴ
47 A	ἄν σε	ἂν σὲ

Readings of B.	The present edition.
47 B δηλαδή	δῆλα δή
ἢ εἰ	ἢ ᾖ (fam. sec.)
(corr. sec. manus)	
47 D ἢ τῇ τοῦ ἑνός	ἢ τῇ τοῦ ἑνός
(corr. sec. manus)	
ἀκολουθήσωμεν (?)	ἀκολουθήσομεν (fam. sec.)
47 E ἢ οὐχί;	ἢ οὐχί;
(corr. sec. manus)	
ἢ φαυλότερον	ἢ φαυλότερον
48 A ἀλλ' ὅτι	ἀλλ' ὅ τι
48 B δηλαδή	δῆλα δή
τῷ καὶ πρότερον	καὶ πρότερον
48 E πεῖσαί σε ταῦτα πράττειν, ἀλλὰ μὴ ἄκοντος	πεῖσαί σε, ἀλλὰ μὴ ἄκοντος ταῦτα πράττειν
49 A ᾖ (saepius: corr. sec. ma-nus)	ἢ
ὡμολογήθη; ὅπερ καὶ ἄρτι ἐλέγετο· ἢ πᾶσαι	ὡμολογήθη; ἢ πᾶσαι
τηλικοίδε γέροντες ἄνδρες	τηλικοίδε ἄνδρες
49 B οὐδαμῶς ἄρα	οὐδαμῶς ἄρα
50 A ἢ οὔ;	ἢ οὔ;
(corr. sec. manus)	
50 B ἰσχύωσιν	ἰσχύουσιν
τὰς δικασθείσας	τὰς δίκας τὰς δικασθείσας (fam.
(corr. sec. manus)	sec.)
50 C ἢ καὶ ταῦτα	ἢ καὶ ταῦτα (fam. sec.)
ἢ ἐμμένειν	ἢ ἐμμένειν
(corr. sec. manus)	
50 E ἆρ' ἐξ ἴσου	ἆρ' ἐξ ἴσου
ἢ πρὸς μὲν ἄρα	ἢ πρὸς μὲν ἄρα
51 A πρὸς δὲ τὴν πατρίδα ἄρα	πρὸς δὲ τὴν πατρίδα ἄρα
ἐξέσται	ἔσται
ἐάν σε	ἐὰν σὲ
51 C ἢ τὸ δίκαιον (?)	ᾖ τὸ δίκαιον
ἢ οὔ; (corr. sec. manus)	ἢ οὔ;
51 D ——————	καὶ οὐδεὶς ἡμῶν τῶν νόμων ἐμπο-δών ἐστιν οὐδ' ἀπαγορεύει, ἐάν τε τις βούληται "om. B, in marg. manu satis vetusta add. b." Sch.
53 A καταγέλαστός τε	καταγέλαστός γε (fam. sec.)
53 B τῶν αὐτῶν πόλεων	τῶν αὐτῶν πόλεων (fam. sec.)
53 D καταλλάξας	μεταλλάξας (fam. sec.)
(corr. in marg. sec. manus)	
54 B οὔτε ὁσιώτερον	οὐδὲ ὁσιώτερον (fam. sec.)

INDEX.

The numbers refer to the pages.

ὦ omitted with vocatives 71

ὡς = 'for' 37

ὡς not = 'although' 29

ὡς ἀληθῶς 43

ὡς ἐγὼ οἶμαι 34

ὡς ἔπος εἰπεῖν 75

ὥσπερ with a prep. in similes 41

CAMBRIDGE : PRINTED BY JOHN CLAY, M.A. AT THE UNIVERSITY PRESS.

THE PITT PRESS SERIES

AND THE

CAMBRIDGE SERIES FOR SCHOOLS

AND TRAINING COLLEGES.

Volumes of the latter series are marked by a dagger †.

COMPLETE LIST

GREEK

Author	Work	Editor	Price
Aeschylus	Prometheus Vinctus	Rackham	2/6
Aristophanes	Aves—Plutus—Ranae	Green	3/6 *each*
,,	Nubes, Vespae	Graves	3/6 *each*
,,	Acharnians	,,	3/-
,,	Peace	,,	3/6
Demosthenes	Olynthiacs	Glover	2/6
,,	Philippics I, II, III	G. A. Davies	2/6
Euripides	Alcestis	Hadley	2/6
,,	Hecuba	Hadley	2/6
,,	Helena	Pearson	3/6
,,	Heraclidae	Pearson	3/6
,,	Hercules Furens	Gray & Hutchinson	2/-
,,	Hippolytus	Hadley	2/-
,,	Iphigeneia in Aulis	Headlam	2/6
,,	Medea	,,	2/6
,,	Orestes	Wedd	4/6
,,	Phoenissae	Pearson	4/-
Herodotus	Book I	Sleeman	4/-
,,	,, V	Shuckburgh	3/-
,,	,, IV, VI, VIII, IX	,,	4/- *each*
,,	,, IX 1—89	,,	2/6
Homer	Odyssey IX, X	Edwards	2/6 *each*
,,	,, XXI	,,	2/-
,,	,, XI	Nairn	2/-
,,	Iliad VI, XXII, XXIII, XXIV	Edwards	2/- *each*
,,	Iliad IX and X	Lawson	2/6
Lucian	Somnium, Charon, etc.	Heitland	3/6
,,	Menippus and Timon	Mackie	3/6
Plato	Apologia Socratis	Adam	3/6
,,	Crito, Euthyphro	,,	2/6 *each*
,,	Protagoras	J. & A. M. Adam	4/6
Plutarch	Demosthenes	Holden	4/6
,,	Gracchi	,,	6/-
,,	Nicias	,,	5/-
,,	Sulla	,,	6/-
,,	Timoleon	,,	6/-

50000

GREEK *continued*

Author	Work	Editor	Price
Sophocles	Oedipus Tyrannus	Jebb	4/-
Thucydides	Book III	Spratt	5/-
,,	Book VI	,,	6/-
,,	Book VII	Holden	5/-
Xenophon	Agesilaus	Hailstone	2/6
,,	Anabasis I–II	Pretor	4/-
,,	,, I, III, IV, V	,,	2/- each
,,	,, II, VI, VII	,,	2/6 each
† ,,	,, I, II, III, IV, V, VI	Edwards	1/6 each
	(*With complete vocabularies*)		
,,	Hellenics I–II	,,	3/6
,,	Cyropaedeia I	Shuckburgh	2/6
,,	,, II	,,	2/-
,,	,, III, IV, V	Holden	5/-
,,	,, VI, VII, VIII	,,	5/-
,,	Memorabilia I, II	Edwards	2/6 each

LATIN

*The volumes marked * contain vocabularies*

Author	Work	Editor	Price
Bede	Eccl. History III, IV	Mayor & Lumby	7/6
Caesar	De Bello Gallico		
	Com. I, III, VI, VIII	Peskett	1/6 each
	,, II–III, and VII	,,	2/- each
	,, I–III	,,	3/-
*† ,,	,, IV–V	,,	1/6
,,	,, I, II, III, IV, V, VI, VII	Shuckburgh	1/6 each
,,	De Bello Gallico. Bk I	,,	-/9
	(*With vocabulary only. no notes*)		
,,	De Bello Gallico. Bk VII		-/8
	(*Text only*)		
,,	De Bello Civili. Com. I	Peskett	3/-
,,	,, ,, Com. III	,,	2/6
Cicero	Actio Prima in C. Verrem	Cowie	1/6
,,	De Amicitia, De Senectute	Reid	3/6 each
,,	De Officiis. Bk III	Holden	2/-
,,	Pro Lege Manilia	Nicol	1/6
,,	Div. in Q. Caec. et Actio Prima in C. Verrem	Heitland & Cowie	3/-
,,	Ep. ad Atticum. Lib. II	Pretor	3/-
,,	Orations against Catiline	Nicol	2/6
*† ,,	In Catilinam I	Flather	1/6
,,	Philippica Secunda	Peskett	3/6
,,	Pro Archia Poeta	Reid	2/-
,,	,, Balbo	,,	1/6
,,	,, Milone	Reid	2/6
,,	,, Murena	Heitland	3/-
,,	,, Plancio	Holden	4/6
,,	,, Roscio	Nicol	2/6
,,	,, Sulla	Reid	3/6
* ,,	Somnium Scipionis	Pearman	2/-
,,	Easy selections from correspondence	Duff	1/6

LATIN *continued*

Author	Work	Editor	Price
*Cornelius Nepos	Four parts	Shuckburgh	1/6 each
*Erasmus	Colloquia Latina	G. M. Edwards	1/6
,,	Colloquia Latina	,,	-/9
	(*With vocabulary only: no notes*)		
* ,,	Altera Colloquia Latina	,,	1/6
Horace	Epistles. Bk I	Shuckburgh	2/6
,,	Odes and Epodes	Gow	5/-
,,	Odes. Books I, III	,,	2/- each
,,	,, Books II, IV; Epodes	,,	1/6 each
,,	Satires. Book I	,,	2/-
,,	,, ,, II	,,	2/-
Juvenal	Satires	Duff	5/-
Livy	Book I	H. J. Edwards	In the Press
,,	,, II	Conway	2/6
,,	,, IV, XXVII	Stephenson	2/6 each
,,	,, V	Whibley	2/6
,,	,, VI	Marshall	2/6
,,	,, IX	Anderson	2/6
,,	,, XXI, XXII	Dimsdale	2/6 each
* ,, (adapted from)	Story of the Kings of Rome	G. M. Edwards	1/6
,,	,, ,, ,, (*With vocabulary only: no notes*)		-/8
* ,, ,,	Horatius and other Stories	,,	1/6
,,	,, ,, ,, (*With vocabulary only: no notes*)		-/9
,,	Exercises on Edwards's The Story of the Kings of Rome	Caldecott	-/6 net
Lucan	Pharsalia. Bk I	Heitland & Haskins	1/6
,,	De Bello Civili. Bk VII	Postgate	2/-
Lucretius	Books III and V	Duff	2/- each
Ovid	Fasti. Book VI	Sidgwick	1/6
,,	Metamorphoses, Bk I	Dowdall	1/6
,,	,, Bk VIII	Summers	1/6
* ,,	Phaethon and other stories	G. M. Edwards	1/6
*† ,,	Selections from the Tristia	Simpson	1/6
*†Phaedrus	Fables. Bks I and II	Flather	1/6
Plautus	Epidicus	Gray	3/-
,,	Stichus	Fennell	2/6
,,	Trinummus	Gray	3/6
Pliny	Letters. Book VI	Duff	2/6
Quintus Curtius	Alexander in India	Heitland & Raven	3/6
Sallust	Catiline	Summers	2/-
,,	Jugurtha	,,	2/6
Tacitus	Agricola and Germania	Stephenson	3/-
,,	Histories. Bk I	Davies	2/6
,,	,, Bk III	Summers	2/6
Terence	Hautontimorumenos	Gray	3/-
Vergil	Aeneid I to XII	Sidgwick	1/6 each
*† ,,	,, I, II, III, V, VI, IX, X, XI, XII	,,	1/6 each
,,	Bucolics	,,	1/6
,,	Georgics I, II, and III, IV	,,	2/- each
,,	Complete Works, Vol. I, Text	,,	3/6
,,	,, ,, Vol. II, Notes	,,	4/6
,,	Opera Omnia	B. H. Kennedy	3/6

FRENCH

*The volumes marked * contain vocabularies*

Author	Work	Editor	Price
About	Le Roi des Montagnes	Ropes	2/-
Balzac	Le Médecin de Campagne	Payen Payne	3/-
*Biart	Quand j'étais petit, Pts I, II	Boïelle	2/- *each*
Boileau	L'Art Poétique	Nichol Smith	2/6
Corneille	Polyeucte	Braunholtz	2/-
,,	Le Cid	Eve	2/-
De Bonnechose	Lazare Hoche	Colbeck	2/-
,,	Bertrand du Guesclin	Leathes	2/-
* ,,	,, Part II		1/6
D'Harleville	Le Vieux Célibataire	Masson	2/-
Delavigne	Louis XI	Eve	2/-
,,	Les Enfants d'Edouard		2/-
De Lamartine	Jeanne d'Arc	Clapin & Ropes	1/6
De Vigny	La Canne de Jonc	Eve	1/6
*Dumas	La Fortune de D'Artagnan	Ropes	2/-
*Enault	Le Chien du Capitaine	Verrall	2/-
,,	,, (*With vocabulary only: no notes*)		-/9
Erckmann-Chatrian	La Guerre	Clapin	3/-
,,	Waterloo, Le Blocus	Ropes	3/- *each*
,,	Madame Thérèse	,,	3/-
,,	Histoire d'un Conscrit	,,	3/-
,,	Exercises on 'Waterloo'	Wilson-Green	1/-
Gautier	Voyage en Italie (Selections)	Payen Payne	3/-
Guizot	Discours sur l'Histoire de la Révolution d'Angleterre	Eve	2/6
Hugo	Les Burgraves	,,	2/6
,,	Selected Poems		
Lemercier	Frédégonde et Brunehaut	Masson	2/-
*Malot	Remi et ses Amis	Verrall	2/-
* ,,	Remi en Angleterre	,,	2/-
Mérimée	Colomba (*Abridged*)	Ropes	2/-
Michelet	Louis XI & Charles the Bold	,,	2/6
Molière	Le Bourgeois Gentilhomme	Clapin	1/6
,,	L'École des Femmes	Saintsbury	2/6
,,	Les Précieuses ridicules	Braunholtz	2/-
,,	,, (*Abridged edition*)	,,	1/-
,,	Le Misanthrope	,,	2/6
,,	L'Avare	,,	2/6
*Perrault	Fairy Tales	Rippmann	1/6
,,	,, (*With vocabulary only: no notes*)	,,	-/9
Piron	La Métromanie	Masson	2/-
Ponsard	Charlotte Corday	Ropes	2/-
Racine	Les Plaideurs	Braunholtz	2/-
,,	,, (*Abridged edition*)	,,	1/-
,,	Athalie	Eve	2/-
Saintine	Picciola	Ropes	2/-
Sandeau	Mdlle de la Seiglière	,,	2/-
Scribe & Legouvé	Bataille de Dames	Bull	2/-
Scribe	Le Verre d'Eau	Colbeck	2/-

FRENCH *continued*

Author	Work	Editor	Price
Sédaine	Le Philosophe sans le savoir	Bull	2/-
Souvestre	Un Philosophe sous les Toits	Eve	2/-
,,	Le Serf & Le Chevrier de Lorraine	Ropes	2/-
*Souvestre	Le Serf	Ropes	1/6
,,		,,	-/9
	(*With vocabulary only: no notes*)		
Spencer	French Verse for upper forms		3/-
Staël, Mme de	Le Directoire	Masson & Prothero	2/-
,,	Dix Années d'Exil (Book II chapters 1—8)	,,	2/-
Thierry	Lettres sur l'histoire de France (XIII—XXIV)	,,	2/6
,,	Récits des Temps Mérovingiens, I—III	Masson & Ropes	3/-
Voltaire	Histoire du Siècle de Louis XIV, in three parts	Masson & Prothero	2/6 *each*
Xavier de Maistre	{ La Jeune Sibérienne. Le Lépreux de la Cité d'Aoste }	Masson	1/6

GERMAN

*The volumes marked * contain vocabularies*

Author	Work	Editor	Price
*Andersen	Eight Stories	Rippmann	2/6
Benedix	Dr Wespe	Breul	3/-
Freytag	Der Staat Friedrichs des Grossen	Wagner	2/-
,,	Die Journalisten	Eve	2/6
Goethe	Knabenjahre (1749—1761)	Wagner & Cartmell	2/-
,,	Hermann und Dorothea	,, ,,	3/6
,,	Iphigenie auf Tauris	Breul	3/6
*Grimm	Twenty Stories	Rippmann	3/-
Gutzkow	Zopf und Schwert	Wolstenholme	3/6
Hackländer	Der geheime Agent	Milner Barry	3/-
Hauff	Das Bild des Kaisers	Breul	3/-
,,	Das Wirthshaus im Spessart	Schlottmann & Cartmell	3/-
*,,	Die Karavane	Schlottmann	3/-
,,	Der Scheik von Alessandria	Rippmann	2/6
Immermann	Der Oberhof	Wagner	3/-
*Klee	Die deutschen Heldensagen	Wolstenholme	3/-
Kohlrausch	Das Jahr 1813	Cartmell	2/-
Lessing	Minna von Barnhelm	Wolstenholme	3/-
Lessing & Gellert	Selected Fables	Breul	3/-
Raumer	Der erste Kreuzzug	Wagner	2/-
Riehl	Culturgeschichtliche Novellen	Wolstenholme	3/-
*,,	Die Ganerben & Die Gerechtigkeit Gottes	,,	3/-
Schiller	Wilhelm Tell	Breul	2/6
,,	,, (*Abridged edition*)	,,	1/6

GERMAN *continued*

Author	Work	Editor	Price
Schiller	Geschichte des dreissigjährigen Kriegs. Book III.	Breul	3/-
,,	Maria Stuart	,,	3/6
,,	Wallenstein I.	,,	3/6
,,	Wallenstein II.	,,	3/6
Sybel	Prinz Eugen von Savoyen	Quiggin	2/6
Uhland	Ernst, Herzog von Schwaben	Wolstenholme	3/6
	German Dactylic Poetry	Wagner	3/-
	Ballads on German History	,,	2/-

SPANISH

Cervantes	La Ilustre Fregona &c.	Kirkpatrick	3/6
Le Sage & Isla	Los Ladrones de Asturias	Kirkpatrick	3/-
Galdós	Trafalgar	,,	4/-

ENGLISH

Author	Work	Editor	Price
	Historical Ballads	Sidgwick	1/6
	Old Ballads	,,	1/6
	English Patriotic Poetry	Salt	1/-
Bacon	History of the Reign of King Henry VII	Lumby	3/-
,,	Essays	West	3/6
,,	New Atlantis	G. C. M. Smith	1/6
Burke	American Speeches	Innes	3/-
Chaucer	Prologue and Knight's Tale	M. Bentinck-Smith	2/6
,,	Clerkes Tale and Squires Tale	Winstanley	2/6
Cowley	Prose Works	Lumby	4/-
Defoe	Robinson Crusoe, Part I	Masterman	2/-
Earle	Microcosmography	West	3/- & 4/-
Goldsmith	Traveller and Deserted Village	Murison	1/6
Gray	Poems	Tovey	4/-
† ,,	Ode on the Spring and The Bard	,,	8d.
† ,,	Ode on the Spring and The Elegy	,,	8d.
Kingsley	The Heroes	E. A. Gardner	1/6
Lamb	Tales from Shakespeare. 2 Series	Flather	1/6 each
Macaulay	Lord Clive	Innes	1/6
,,	Warren Hastings	,,	1/6
,,	William Pitt and Earl of Chatham	,,	2/6
† ,,	John Bunyan	,,	1/-
† ,,	John Milton	Flather	1/6
,,	Lays and other Poems		1/6
,,	History of England Chaps. I—III	Reddaway	2/-
Mayor	A Sketch of Ancient Philosophy from Thales to Cicero		3/6
,,	Handbook of English Metre		2/-
Milton	Arcades	Verity	1/6
,,	Ode on the Nativity, L'Allegro, Il Penseroso & Lycidas	,,	2/6
† ,,	Comus & Lycidas	,,	2/-
,,	Comus	,,	1/-
,,	Samson Agonistes	,,	2/6
,,	Sonnets	,,	1/6

ENGLISH *continued*

Author	Work	Editor	Price
Milton	Paradise Lost, six parts	Verity	2/- *each*
More	History of King Richard III	Lumby	3/6
,,	Utopia	,,	2/-
Pope	Essay on Criticism	West	2/-
Scott	Marmion	Masterman	2/6
,,	Lady of the Lake	,,	2/6
,,	Lay of the last Minstrel	Flather	2/-
,,	Legend of Montrose	Simpson	2/6
,,	Lord of the Isles	Flather	2/-
,,	Old Mortality	Nicklin	2/6
,,	Kenilworth	Flather	2/6
,,	The Talisman	A. S. Gaye	2/-
,,	Quentin Durward	Murison	2/-
Shakespeare	A Midsummer-Night's Dream	Verity	1/6
,,	Twelfth Night	,,	1/6
,,	Julius Caesar	,,	1/6
,,	The Tempest	,,	1/6
,,	King Lear	,,	1/6
,,	Merchant of Venice	,,	1/6
,,	King Richard II	,,	1/6
,,	As You Like It	,,	1/6
,,	King Henry V	,,	1/6
,,	Macbeth	,,	1/6
,,	Hamlet	,,	1/6
Shakespeare & Fletcher	Two Noble Kinsmen	Skeat	3/6
Sidney	An Apologie for Poetrie	Shuckburgh	3/-
Spenser	Fowre Hymnes	Miss Winstanley	2/-
Tennyson	Fifty Poems, 1830—1864	Lobban	2/6
Wordsworth	Selected Poems	Miss Thomson	1/6
West	Elements of English Grammar		2/6
,,	English Grammar for Beginners		1/-
,,	Key to English Grammars		3/6 *net*
Carlos	Short History of British India		1/-
Mill	Elementary Commercial Geography		1/6
Bartholomew	Atlas of Commercial Geography		3/-
Robinson	Church Catechism Explained		2/-
Jackson	The Prayer Book Explained. Part I		2/6

MATHEMATICS

Ball	Elementary Algebra		4/6
†Blythe	Geometrical Drawing		
	Part I		2/6
	Part II		2/-
Euclid	Books I—VI, XI, XII	H. M. Taylor	5/-
,,	Books I—VI	,,	4/-
,,	Books I—IV	,,	3/-
	Also separately		
,,	Books I, & II; III, & IV; V, & VI; XI, & XII 1/6 *each*		
,,	Solutions to Exercises in Taylor's		
	Euclid	W. W. Taylor	10/6

MATHEMATICS *continued*

Author	Work	Editor	Price
	And separately		
Euclid	Solutions to Bks I—IV	W. W. Taylor	6/-
,,	Solutions to Books VI. XI	,,	6/-
Hobson & Jessop	Elementary Plane Trigonometry		4/6
Loney	Elements of Statics and Dynamics		7/6
	Part I. Elements of Statics		4/6
	,, II. Elements of Dynamics		3/6
,,	Elements of Hydrostatics		4/6
,,	Solutions to Examples, Hydrostatics		5/-
,,	Solutions of Examples, Statics and Dynamics		7/6
,,	Mechanics and Hydrostatics		4/6
Smith, C.	Arithmetic for Schools, with or without answers		3/6
,,	Part I. Chapters I—VIII. Elementary, with or without answers		2/-
,,	Part II. Chapters IX—XX, with or without answers		2/-
Hale, G.	Key to Smith's Arithmetic		7/6

EDUCATIONAL SCIENCE

†Bidder & Baddeley	Domestic Economy		4/6
†Bosanquet	{ The Education of the Young from the *Republic* of Plato }		2/6
†Burnet	Aristotle on Education		2/6
Comenius	Life and Educational Works	S. S. Laurie	3/6
Farrar	General Aims of the Teacher }		1/6
Poole	Form Management } 1 vol.		
†Hope & Browne	A Manual of School Hygiene		3/6
Locke	Thoughts on Education	R. H. Quick	3/6
†MacCunn	The Making of Character		2/6
Milton	Tractate on Education	O. Browning	2/-
Sidgwick	On Stimulus		1/-
Thring	Theory and Practice of Teaching		4/6

†Woodward	A Short History of the Expansion of the British Empire (1500—1902)	4/-
† ,,	An Outline History of the British Empire (1500—1902)	1/6 *net*

CAMBRIDGE UNIVERSITY PRESS

𝕷𝖔𝖓𝖉𝖔𝖓: FETTER LANE, E.C.

C. F. CLAY, MANAGER

𝕰𝖉𝖎𝖓𝖇𝖚𝖗𝖌𝖍: 100, PRINCES STREET